Ask Your
Mortgage Broker

Ask Your Mortgage Broker

The Most Practical Guide for Canadian Homebuyers and Homeowners

Blair Anderson

INSOMNIAC PRESS

Library and Archives Canada Cataloguing in Publication

Anderson, Blair, 1963-
    Ask your mortgage broker : the most practical guide for Canadian homebuyers and homeowners / Blair Anderson.

ISBN 978-1-55483-027-5

    1. Mortgage brokers--Canada. 2. House buying--Canada. 3. Home ownership--Canada. I. Title.

HG2040.5.C2A75 2011   332.7'20971   C2011-905336-5

The publisher gratefully acknowledges the support of the Department of Canadian Heritage through the Canada Book Fund.

Printed and bound in Canada

Insomniac Press
520 Princess Ave.
London, ON N6B 2B8
www.insomniacpress.com

In memory of my father, Howard M. Anderson

And for my mother, Ann M. Anderson

CONTENTS

FOREWORD

The fact that Blair Anderson put in the effort to write this book says a lot about him. As a practicing real estate lawyer, I have witnessed firsthand the honesty, intelligence, and plain hard slogging that Blair has always brought to the table for his clients.

Here he is now, having put so much time and effort into a book that will likely do a lot of good for others, while for him, it provides only the satisfaction of a job well done—no appearances on Oprah, no glory, and no great financial reward.

Many mortgage brokers are a credit to their calling; though, as Blair points out, some are not. So many of my clients who have had problems with their lenders and their loans—some even resulting in eviction—could have avoided them had they read this book.

I congratulate Blair for writing it, and I will be keeping copies in my waiting room as a great asset to give to my clients.

Peter Cass
Cass & Bishop Barristers & Solicitors
Burlington, Ontario, Canada

PREFACE

Since 1992, I have been working in the Canadian mortgage industry, the majority of that time as a mortgage broker. When I sit down with clients at my office, or speak to them by phone, I routinely educate them on my role as a mortgage broker and the benefits of using me. Why? Most of the time because I get questions such as, "Are there any hidden costs for using a mortgage broker? How are you paid? Why shouldn't I deal directly with the bank?" These are all good questions, which I am only too happy to answer.

The problem is, in the nineteen years since I began my career, I expected the fog to clear and consumers to gain a better understanding about mortgage brokers. The sad truth is, as an industry, we have failed to adequately educate the public about our role. This is one of the reasons why I decided to write this book. There has been, and still remains, very little written about this misunderstood and under-used resource in a Canadian context.

Ask your Mortgage Broker can best be described as an exposé of the Canadian mortgage broker industry's history, utilitarianism, and best-kept secrets. I consider it a must-read for every existing or potential homeowner.

INTRODUCTION

If we consider Darwin's theory of natural selection, it can be argued that those who prevail are those who learn to collaborate and improvise most effectively. The mortgage business is a good example of that. There are many players, including lenders, mortgage brokers, governments, appraisers, realtors, lawyers, insurance brokers, home inspectors, and last but not least, you, the consumer. Mortgage participants who learn to collaborate and adjust to the business environment will prevail. Those who don't, may become roadkill.

I wrote this book with two mortgage participants in mind: the consumer and the apprentice mortgage broker eager to learn the trade. I have stood in both your shoes and I understand the uneasy feeling as you stand at the doorway, looking to begin your quest for success!

The supply of reference books has not kept up with today's information-hungry consumer. Most of the available information comes from the lending community and offers only a basic overview of mortgage underwriting. There is also a bias regarding where to go to apply for a mortgage. The Canada Mortgage and Housing Corporation (CMHC) has written more technical material with greater objectivity, but nothing I have seen provides the depth and objective insight you will need to adequately erase that uneasy feeling of applying for a mortgage or starting your career as a mortgage broker.

This book is based on real-life stories and hands-on experience over the last nineteen years. At the very least, as you go through this book and pay attention to the details, you'll learn how diverse a species we are and how every consumer needs to understand their own unique set of circumstances before accepting some cookie-cutter arrangement for a mortgage.

This book is organized to cover key areas about mortgages and the business of obtaining one. Each chapter stands independently but is linked to the others. If you know little about mortgages, you should read the chapters sequentially to appreciate the industry's background and to follow the information from a basic to a more advanced level.

Chapters 6, 7, 8, and 10 contain invaluable information about the industry's landscape. From key advisors and industry associations, you will come to know the practice of referrals, the methods of broker compensation, the legislated disclosure requirements, and the industry's goal to be self-regulated. The final chapters take a practical look at the process of buying and selling a home and look at *all* the costs. I also added one last chapter on private mortgages, given their rise in activity since the 2008 credit crunch and the subsequent contraction in institutional subprime lenders.

Come walk a mile in my shoes. I hope the wisdom you gain will dull the pain the next time you ask yourself, "How will I pay for that?"

Chapter 1

A History of Mortgage Brokering in Ontario

In 1992, I bought my first house. The financial experience seemed to have had a profound and lasting impression on me, so much so that I quit my job as a junior stockbroker in downtown Toronto to become a junior mortgage broker. My timing wasn't the best. Taking out a mortgage in April and quitting my job in July didn't place me in good favour with my wife, but I was young and full of confidence. I thought I had finally found my calling. Nineteen years later, I'm still at it. I guess I was right this time. I also married an incredibly generous and patient woman—thank you, Michelle.

Let me take you back to an earlier time when the mortgage broker industry was still in its infancy. Since my career started and remains based in Ontario, I cannot speak in detail to the industry's development in other parts of Canada. However, my feeling is Ontario likely resembles the development of the industry in most other provinces. It's important to know a little about the history of mortgage brokers if you are going to build enough trust to work with one.

Since the industry has evolved so much over time, it's easy for the unwary to be misled by the misconceptions and misinformation still present in the marketplace today. Furthermore, purchasing a home is likely the most money you will ever spend at one time and the process involves working with a few trusted advisors, including a mortgage broker. You owe it to yourself to both know how they operate and know what they bring to the table. By understanding their history, you will achieve both.

Before any laws or regulations were established in the industry, real estate lawyers were the only ones acting as mortgage brokers. Many of them had wealthy clients willing to loan money to borrowers who could not obtain financing through banks. As time passed, without any regulations and no requirements to become a mortgage broker, the industry quickly attracted new talent. Unfortunately, many of the newcomers were underqualified and unscrupulous.

As the industry grew, the reputation of mortgage brokers became less appealing. Labels such as "loan sharks" or "lender of last resort" were common. The business of mortgage brokers was rooted in the subprime mortgage market. That is, the practice of lending money in situations that didn't meet the "prime" lending criteria of conservative financial institutions. Some of these situations included borrowers having damaged credit, borrowers being unable to prove their income on paper, properties being out of the way/less marketable, etc. Any situation that didn't conform to "prime" underwriting guidelines fell into the category of subprime lending, which is also known as non-conforming or alternative lending.

The marketplace needs and can support a healthy subprime lending market. Any one of us can have an unforeseen change in financial circumstances or may be seeking financing under difficult terms that don't meet the strict lending criteria of conservative banks. Where things went wrong in the beginning for mortgage brokers was the way in which they conducted themselves in this new budding industry of subprime lending. In the absence of a safety net of regulations, whether policed by government or a private self-regulatory body, conduct unbecoming a professional will and did occur.

NEW LEGISLATION FOR MORTGAGE BROKERS

For mortgage brokers, after years of using unsavoury boiler room tactics and exploiting borrowers—leading them to think their situation was far less bankable than it really was in order to justify unethical and exorbitant broker fees—the tipping point came in 1960 when the Government of Ontario introduced the *Mortgage Brokers Act*.

The government designed the act to help eliminate unethical conduct and root out any bad apples, but it had little influence and a significant shortage of staff to properly police it. It did little to curb bad behaviour. When I entered the industry in 1992, more than thirty years after the act was introduced, only two enforcement officers were employed by the Ministry of Finance to conduct audits on individual brokerage houses. During this time in Ontario, 791 mortgage brokers were registered under the act. This is not a good ratio for reining in bad behaviour.

Consequently, the act needed changes made to it, which first came in 1990 and included improved standards for full disclosure to the consumer and stiffer penalties for non-compliance. There was also a change of guard. The government hired a new registrar named William Vasiliou with a clear mandate to clean up the industry. During his tenure, Vasiliou managed to close down an unprecedented number of brokerage houses for non-compliance with the act. This isn't a job for the weak-hearted. During my post-graduate studies at Seneca College, Vasiliou was my instructor for my course in ethics. I worked my ass off in that course just to get a C. I'm sure he was a nice guy away from the business, but after years of ruling over the industry in the office of the Registrar of Mortgage Brokers, both in and out of court, he had set the bar high for us neophytes.

The efforts to clean up the industry started to gain momentum during this time as prime lending institutions also became interested in using the mortgage broker community for originating new "prime" business. Mortgage brokers now had access to both the subprime and prime lending communities. Of the growing number of prime lending institutions signing up to do business with mortgage brokers, TD was the first of the Big Five banks get on board.

EDUCATIONAL REFORM

Real change started to occur when the educational requirements for becoming a mortgage broker significantly changed in 1995. The aforementioned post-graduate program was established at Seneca College, comprised of fifteen courses over two semesters. Upon graduation, another two years of working experience in the industry was required before you could apply for your broker's license. With much improved qualifications, the rest of the prime lending community began hitching their wagons to the mortgage broker community. But let's not kid ourselves. Lower operating costs and profitability would have been one of the main reasons the banks agreed to use mortgage brokers, but the banks also needed to know mortgage brokers had reached a new standard in ethics and professionalism. More important, however, was to have the Canadian consumer accept that mortgage brokers would represent the banks.

Before establishing a comprehensive post-graduate program, obtaining your mortgage broker license was no more difficult than completing a one-weekend course, including passing a written test, and then applying to the Ministry for your license. This was not the formidable entry you would associate with any profession, and it's little wonder banks were reluctant to work with mortgage brokers in the beginning. In fact, the banks and other industry stakeholders were instrumental in establishing the course material that became the new standard for mortgage brokers in the industry.

The fifteen courses that make up the mandatory post-graduate program give aspiring students the proper background they need to start their career as a professional mortgage broker. But like any apprenticeship, additional time in the field is a must before the Ministry can confidently issue a license. The current two years' experience is a safe minimum. This new standard for mortgage brokers puts the industry on par with other financial service professionals such as insurance brokers, real estate brokers, financial planners, etc.

Mortgage brokers who received their license before the new legislation were allowed to be grandfathered. What some may lack in a formal education they make up for in experience. When shopping around for a mortgage broker, be sure you ask when they received their license. For those who received theirs before 1997, be sure to be otherwise satisfied with their qualifications before considering having one represent you.

MORTGAGE BROKER COMPENSATION

When I started my career as a mortgage broker in 1992, the subprime lending community scarcely resembled the market it is today. The lenders participating in this arena didn't pay brokers a commission for the clients we brought to them. It was as though we should be grateful that they would fund the deal at all. Consequently, our only compensation came from charging the client a broker fee.

With only a limited number of lenders competing for this riskier business, the lenders doing the deals could pretty much charge whatever interest rate they wanted. They would also typically charge the borrower a lender's fee. Again, they would not pay the broker one dime for the business. What the lender's fee and broker's fee looked like depended on how difficult the deal was to place and the time required to put it together. Some borrowers come with a lot more work than others do.

The worst-case scenario for the borrower would be if the mortgage had to be placed with a private lender. If a financial institution in the subprime market deemed the deal too risky to fund, it would be left to a private lender, who would price it accordingly. For example, the table below shows how a private lender's first mortgage might compare to a bank's first mortgage:

Private Lender vs. Bank

Terms	Private	Bank
First mortgage amount	$100,000	$100,000
Lender fee (1% of mortgage)	$1,000	n/a
Broker fee (1% of mortgage)	$1,000	n/a
ILA (independent legal advice)	$250	n/a
Interest rate	10%	5%
Monthly mortgage payment	$894.49	$581.60

From the borrower's perspective, using a mortgage broker for a subprime mortgage meant high interest rates and many fees. The preceding sentence represents the interminable stigma that mortgage brokers have carried to the present day. As you will see, this badge of dishonour does not represent today's modern mortgage broker. We should leave it in the past. With ever-growing competition in the prime marketplace, however, some would rather keep it around.

By the late '90s, competition in the subprime market began to blossom. Each year, another lender would arrive. What happened next made jaws drop everywhere across the industry. Subprime lenders, now competing hard for the lucrative business, started paying mortgage brokers a commission akin to the prime lending institutions. Competition is a beautiful thing. Today, most of the subprime lenders pay as much or more compensation to the broker than any prime lender does.

This put mortgage brokers in a precarious position. Brokering subprime mortgages now represented two income sources for the mortgage broker: a broker fee paid by the borrower and a commission paid by the lender. How would brokers balance the two? The answer, of course, was at the discretion of the mortgage broker. The only restriction then and now on broker fees falls under Canadian law. Section 347 of the *Criminal Code* defines the crime of *usury* (called "criminal interest rate") as follows:

> "Criminal rate" means an effective annual rate of interest calculated in accordance with generally accepted actuarial practices and principles that exceeds 60% on the credit advanced under an agreement or arrangement.

From the borrower's perspective, things could only get better. Competition would take care of that. Brokers who still wanted to charge the same amount in fees on deals that now also earned them a commission from lenders risked losing business to the mortgage brokers who were willing to charge less.

My view on this has always been the same. Having worked in

both periods—before and after the time subprime lenders started paying commissions—I know that the extra work involved in putting together subprime mortgages compared to prime mortgages hasn't changed. The extra work brokers do deserves extra compensation. How much more depends on what they consider fair. To that end, all I can say is buyer beware. As recently as 2009, some subprime lenders have contracted with mortgage brokers for the abolition of any broker fees whatsoever. This was the direct result of the notorious few bad apples who were greedy. Again, buyer beware.

PRIME MORTGAGE MARKET

Growth in prime lending was equally intense. Believe it or not, some brokers would charge fees for their service in this area. I suppose they wanted to be compensated for securing favorable terms the borrowers wouldn't be able to obtain on their own, which often meant saving thousands of dollars on the cost of the mortgage. However, once again, competition would take care of this practice. I don't believe very many brokers can get away with this today.

If you are a prime borrower, the rewards are good. Using a mortgage broker will secure you the best rate and terms to match your circumstances and it will cost you nothing for the mortgage broker's service. Moreover, you will also save a lot of time you would have spent talking to various lenders and never getting the same independent objective advice you get from an independent mortgage broker. At the risk of sounding impartial, there is no better path to take for securing your mortgage than through a qualified independent mortgage broker.

But mortgage brokers don't work for free. Even with prime borrowers, when the only compensation comes from the lender, brokers are well paid. The traditional compensation model for mortgage brokers is a "kill and eat" mentality, as some like to call it. That is, lenders pay mortgage brokers a one-time lump sum when the deal closes. The amount depends on the size of the loan and the term taken by the borrowers. Lenders will generally compensate more for the longer terms and less for the shorter terms. It makes sense, right?

If the borrowers take a longer term, the bank will make more money. For example, the table below represents a lender's typical compensation model for the mortgage broker. The dollar amount of compensation is based on a $100,000 mortgage:

Lender Compensation Model for Mortgage Brokers

Mortgage Term (years)	Compensation (basis points)	Compensation (dollar amount)
1	50	$500
2	50	$500
3	50	$500
4	60	$600
5	80	$800

As you can see, the amount of compensation is based on the size of the mortgage. You can see how this would be good news for mortgage brokers who work in a large metropolitan area where the average mortgage size is bigger. And any discussion you have about the mortgage broker's compensation (or fluctuating mortgage rates, for that matter) has to include the term *basis points*.

There are 100 basis points in 1%. It's a handy tool for referring to changes in interest rates outside of the familiar quarter-point increments. For example, a typical press release might say, "All mortgage terms increased by 15 basis points." This means that if the current five-year term was 5.00%, it just went up to 5.15%. The same terminology is used to describe mortgage broker compensation. For example, using the table above, the mortgage broker is paid 80 basis points if the borrowers take a five-year term.

However, the kill-and-eat mentality has its shortcomings, especially for new mortgage brokers trying to establish themselves when revenues in the early months and years can be tenuous. A better revenue model for the mortgage broker would be one that parallels compensation models used in other industries such as the insurance brokerage or financial planning industries. Under those models, a smaller lump sum is paid out on closing and a continual trailer fee or annuity is paid out over the life of the loan.

The trailer fee model has been a long time coming for mortgage brokers but finally arrived in 2004 when Cervus Financial Corp became the first lender offering this compensation model. Since then, only one other lender has followed suit: Merix Financial. Like Cervus, Merix was also new to Canada and looking to establish market share. Therein lies a fundamental problem preventing the adoption of the trailer fee compensation model: lenders with an established market share in Canada don't experience much loss of mortgage business at renewal time.

Surveys have shown that most banks do a good job of keeping mortgage customers once they have acquired them. So why would banks want to continue to pay mortgage brokers for business they are already keeping? Until established banks see a greater loss of business, it's unlikely that things will change. However, market forces will once again have the final say on how this trend continues. As more mortgage brokers gravitate to this revenue model, the banks will have to take notice and act accordingly.

From a mortgage broker's perspective, a consistent revenue model is easier to work with, and when the broker is ready to retire and sell the business, having a known revenue stream will make it much easier to determine its valuation. From a lender's perspective, this would also curtail the practice of mortgage brokers soliciting existing clients at renewal time in an attempt to move clients to another lender just to earn another commission.

MORTGAGE BROKERING OUTSIDE OF ONTARIO

As a final note on legislative change for mortgage brokers in Ontario, on July 1, 2008, approximately forty-eight years after the original *Mortgage Brokers Act*, Ontario adopted the new *Mortgage Brokerages, Lenders and Administrators Act*. The older act could no longer effectively represent the industry, which had fundamentally changed from the early days when mortgage brokers were considered lenders of last resort. Today, mortgage brokers are ambassadors representing all lenders; they are technologically savvy and hold the highest education and ethical standards in the industry. The next stop: self-regulation.

With the exception of Alberta, where mortgage brokers are regulated by a non-government agency, the Real Estate Council of Alberta (RECA), provincial regulations for mortgage brokers falls under the jurisdiction of one of the following government regulators:

- Financial Institutions Commission of British Columbia (FICOM)
- Saskatchewan Financial Services Commission
- Manitoba Securities Commission
- New Brunswick Department of Justice and Consumer Affairs
- Newfoundland Department of Government Services, Financial Services Regulation Division
- Service Nova Scotia and Municipal Relations
- Organisme d'autoréglémentation du courtage immobilier du Québec (OACIQ)

Currently, Prince Edward Island, the Yukon, Northwest Territories, and Nunavut are the only province/territories without any regulations for mortgage brokers.

I expected Ontario's history for mortgage brokers would be similar to the evolution seen in most other provinces. It was born out of a subprime mortgage culture, with real estate lawyers predominately acting as mortgage brokers before any laws and regulations. After all, we know it was much later when the prime lending institutions realized the value of using mortgage brokers as a variable-cost distribution system. To the contrary, however, some provinces, like the four noted above, are still without any regulations.

Similarly, in November 2008, following the financial crises in the U.S., the Government of Manitoba decided to proceed with regulation of the mortgage broker industry. The subsequent *Mortgage Brokers Act* (previously the *Mortgage Dealers Act*) was proclaimed on April 20, 2011, and came into effect on May 1, 2011. The act is now Manitoba law and regulates the activities of mortgage brokers. To become a mortgage broker, the business or individual arranging your mortgage must be registered with the Manitoba Securities Commission. At the time of this writing, they were still processing applications and so didn't have an exact number of licenses issued.

For most other provinces, the history and evolution of the mortgage broker industry followed a similar path and timeline to Ontario's. For example, in 1967, two more provincial legislatures jumped on the bandwagon to provide more consumer protection. Saskatchewan introduced its own *Mortgage Brokers Act*, and Nova Scotia introduced the *Trust and Loans Corporations Act*, legislation that took aim at revealing the true cost of borrowing in dollars and cents.

On October 1, 2010, Saskatchewan introduced the new *Mortgage Brokerages and Mortgage Administrators Act*. As of March 31, 2011, their fiscal year end, Saskatchewan had 277 licensees under the act. The licensees include mortgage brokers, mortgage associates, and mortgage brokerages. One notable change in the new act was the requirement for all applicants for mortgage brokerage and mortgage administrator licenses to obtain errors and omissions insurance in a form approved by the Saskatchewan Superintendent of Financial Institutions.

In 1975, the Government of Newfoundland and Labrador first proclaimed the *Mortgage Brokers Act* and for mainly the same reasons: consumer protection. There are currently eighty-one licenses issued in the province of Newfoundland and Labrador.

In Alberta, the *Mortgage Brokers Regulations Act* was administered from 1964 to 1980 by the Alberta Securities Commission. From 1980 to 1996, administration of the act was transferred to the Government of Alberta under the Superintendent of Real Estate. The Real Estate Council of Alberta (RECA) has been regulating mortgage brokers in Alberta through administration of the *Real Estate Act* since July 1, 1996. As of September 30, 2010, the end of RECA's last fiscal year, they had 2,610 individuals authorized as mortgage brokers or associates.

The last time the *Real Estate Act* underwent significant changes was July 2008; however, there were few changes at that time that related specifically to mortgage brokerage practices. One of the most significant changes occurred recently. Effective September 1, 2011, all Alberta mortgage brokerages must carry errors and omissions insurance with fraud coverage. An identical provision was made for Ontario mortgage brokers on July 1, 2008, when Ontario introduced its new *Mortgage Brokerages, Lenders and Administrators Act*.

In British Columbia, *The Mortgage Brokers Act* was introduced in 1972. There are currently 4,507 individual mortgage brokers and 818 mortgage brokerages licensed under the act.

Changes to the act since its inception have been principally focused on consumer protection. Major changes included the following:

- Before 2000, real estate licensees were deemed to be mortgage brokers and didn't require registration under the *Mortgage Brokers Act* to conduct mortgage broker activity. Since that time, registration has been a requirement.

- In 2000, investor/lender disclosure statements were introduced along with conflict of interest disclosure.

- In 2005, the definition of a mortgage broker was expanded to include "carries on a business of collecting monies secured by mortgages." This means persons administering mortgages are required to be registered under the *Mortgage Brokers Act*.

Beginning in June 2011, British Columbia has taken a lead in licensing reciprocity. Various trade mobility agreements promote cross-provincial labour mobility through the elimination of occupational barriers for mortgage broker registrants or licensees in provincial jurisdictions with qualification requirements. The British Columbia Registrar of Mortgage Brokers currently recognizes the occupational standards of individuals who have qualified for licensing or registration under equivalent or similar legislation in the provinces of Alberta, Saskatchewan, Manitoba, Ontario, and Quebec.

In Quebec, the regulation of mortgage broker activity is a bit more convoluted in terms of the regulating bodies involved and the number of financial intermediaries deemed to be acting as mortgage brokers. For example, insurance and securities representatives can also be involved in activities in connection with loans secured by immovable hypothecs (mortgages). For them, regulation has transfered from the Association des courtiers et agents immobiliers du Québec (ACAIQ) in 1994 to the Autorité des marchés financiers (AMF) in 1999, and then back to the ACAIQ on May 1, 2010. At that time, the ACAIQ was renamed the Organisme d'autoréglementation du courtage immobilier du Québec (OACIQ). The OACIQ is responsible for the application and enforcement of the *Real Estate Brokerage Act*.

In fact, regulation started even before the ACAIQ, when the *Real Estate Brokerage Act* was adopted in 1962. As to the aforementioned transfers between regulatory bodies concerning insurance and securities representatives, in practice, most mortgage brokers and agents continued to be regulated by the ACAIQ. Until May 1, 2010, the *Real Estate Brokerage Act* did not distinguish between real estate agents and mortgage brokers (all were real estate brokers). The new act provides for the issuing of licenses in two fields of practice: real estate brokerage and mortgage brokerage. While the full-service real estate broker will be able to act in residential, commercial, and mortgage matters, the mortgage broker will only be able to act in mortgages. Unless they work on their own accounts, the mortgage broker will only be able to represent a mortgage broker agency, while the real estate broker will be able to represent a real estate agency or a mortgage broker agency. However, it will be possible to hold both types of licenses. There are currently 316 registered mortgage brokerages and 35 agencies.

Under the new May 1, 2010, *Real Estate Brokerage Act*, the OACIQ established competency framework guides to help future mortgage brokers understand what competencies must be developed and mastered in order to act ethically and responsibly in their brokerage practice. New examinations were designed based on these competency frameworks. To view the OACIQ's competency framework guide for mortgage brokers, go to: http://oaciq.com/sites/default/

files/article/fichiers/frameworkmortgage201009.pdf

Unlike some other jurisdictions, New Brunswick doesn't currently have mortgage broker legislation. However, they do require that all brokerages dealing in personal credit and residential mortgages register with the regulator under the *Cost of Credit Disclosure Act*. This legislation deals with the disclosure of the cost of borrowing but doesn't include a licensing scheme. The act was introduced September 15, 2010, and the province has an estimated forty brokerages registered.

For more information about the status or history of mortgage broker regulations in any province, it would be best for you to contact the regulator directly using the above list.

CHAPTER 2

BANK DISTRIBUTION CHANNELS

In the world of mortgage finance, lenders position themselves to *originate* new mortgage business through a number of different *distribution channels*. That's a bit heavy on the industry jargon. In layman's terms, lenders have a number of ways to source new business. Each of these sources—or distribution channels, as the banks like to call them—comes with its own set of operating costs. That's where mortgage brokers come in. They are the most cost effective and efficient operation the banks have for originating, or acquiring, new mortgage business. Compared to the bank's oldest distribution channel (their branch networks), the mortgage broker channel is far less expensive to operate. You can probably guess some of the other distribution channels lenders use:

- Call centres
- Online applications
- Mobile mortgage sales force

Just like the banks' oldest bricks-and-mortar channel, the three newer channels listed above also operate at a higher unit cost or overhead compared to the mortgage broker channel. They do however represent an evolution away from a strictly bricks-and-mortar company to a bricks-and-clicks company, a business model by which a company integrates both an offline (bricks) and an online (clicks) presence—all things to all people, if you will.

In today's modern world, new lenders are opting to drop the bricks component all together and pass the savings along to you. Take, for example, ING Direct, who opened their virtual doors in April 1997 with a television commercial that humbly announced, "We are new here." They offered a safe and simple way to save and borrow that gives you real choice. ING Direct Canada's 2009 year-end reporting posted over 1.6 million clients. By June 30, 2010, they employed 984 full-time people and had over $30.7 billion in assets.

Many more lenders have followed suit since then to set up shop exclusively using the mortgage broker channel. Others have elected to also use the call centre and/or online application channels in addition to the mortgage broker channel. As an example, in 2008, mortgage applications submitted to ING Direct through the mortgage broker channel vs. the call centre channel were unofficially and approximately 70% vs. 30% respectively.

Whether you are buying a home or refinancing your existing mortgage, it's not about dollars and cents exclusively for everyone. Let's look closer at each mortgage distribution channel and see which one is best for you.

THE BRANCH NETWORK

For some consumers, the oldest channel is where they go to do all their banking, including getting a mortgage. For them, this is the most convenient, and they probably have a good relationship with one of the branch representatives. If you have a good relationship with your branch and have a good history of doing business with your branch (e.g. chequing account, savings account, RRSP, personal loan, line of credit, credit cards, etc.), you can leverage that relationship into a good discounted rate on your mortgage. This is referred to as relationship-based pricing, or RBP.

Remember, in the eyes of the big corporate bank, each branch operates as an individual profit centre. If your level of overall business with the branch is good, it means it's good for the branch's bottom line and you should be rewarded for it with RBP. Conversely, if you walk into a branch without this leverage, you can't expect RBP. But how far can RBP go? Remember, you are already starting from the highest unit cost compared to the other channels.

Moreover, branch staff are trained and motivated to make the branch as profitable as possible. This directly affects the bonuses handed out to staff at the end of the year. So don't expect anyone at the branch to be overly generous when it comes to discounting your rate or advising you on any mortgage terms and strategies that will cost them money. Branch managers have limits on how deeply they can discount rates, beyond which requires the approval from their district managers, who discourage the practice. It can be a competitive world inside the banks, between districts and branches, all gunning to be the most profitable. This is something you should keep in mind.

CALL CENTRES AND ONLINE APPLICATIONS

I will lump these two channels together since I am sure they operate in the same way. Essentially, as the consumer, you have two options: either you prefer to talk with someone over the phone when applying for a mortgage or you are happy not to talk with anyone and are comfortable filling out the online application on your own. The latter option would appeal to someone who is relatively confident in what they are applying for and doesn't require any discussion. They are looking for the quickest and easiest approach to getting things done. I would suggest that these consumers might be cutting themselves short in the interest of time. They may feel they have done enough homework on the subject to proceed, but I can assure you there is too much to learn, too much bias, and often too many changes going on in the market (e.g., product specials) to act in haste. Remember the saying, "Haste makes waste."

The former option may put you in touch with a live person, but don't count on that for your salvation. The consumer seeking this option is not much different from the one previously described, except perhaps they are a little less confident. Unfortunately, the live person you will encounter under this approach can best be described as an "order taker." Don't count on any deep and healthy discussion around strategy and product. The online bank representative may be just as knowledgeable as one working inside a branch, but the service and bias remains the same, though perhaps it's a bit more tech savvy.

MOBILE MORTGAGE SALES FORCE

Some consumers are loyal to their bank but want the flexibility to meet a bank representative when and where it suits them. For this consumer, the mobile bank representative is the preferred choice. Early in my career, I worked as a mobile bank representative for one of the major banks. I know first-hand how this channel operates and the good people who choose to work in this capacity. The training, supervising, and expertise behind this channel are second to none.

If you were to call a branch today to make an appointment to come in and speak with someone about a mortgage, some banks would refer you to one of their mobile bank representatives. However, it would be an experience that could leave you scratching your head if you were to walk into a branch unannounced and ask to speak with someone about your mortgage and they sent you away with the name and phone number of someone to call and make an appointment.

It's always a good idea to call ahead. Mobile bank representatives can arrange to meet with you at any branch, at your home, or offsite somewhere such as a donut shop—whatever works for you. Mobile bank representatives also work well beyond branch hours, so finding a time to meet is never a problem.

The problems with using this channel include the obvious bias. No mobile bank representative from ABC bank will ever talk to you about good product alternatives at XYZ bank. Again, this channel operates from a higher unit cost compared to the mortgage broker channel, so it's difficult for them to be as price competitive. Like the branch network, the bank's mobile bank representative channel has its own competitive districts, each looking to maximize their own profitability. That doesn't bode well from the consumer's perspective. Next to the mortgage broker channel, the mobile bank representative channel is the next most cost efficient. Mobile bank representatives also get paid on commission like mortgage brokers, but the channel has its own overhead, including training costs, sales manager and other senior management salaries, outfitting reps with laptops, phones, scanners, etc. These are all costs that don't exist with the mortgage broker channel.

MORTGAGE BROKER CHANNEL

I have already talked about the mortgage broker channel being the most cost effective and efficient operation for originating new business for the banks. It ultimately comes down to the kind of consumer you are. Knowing what you know now in terms of the operating costs associated with lenders originating new mortgage business, what channel do you think will offer you better rates and terms on your mortgage? The mortgage broker channel, hands down!

Getting favourable rates and terms is just one advantage for using a mortgage broker. As an independent unbiased representative working on your behalf, a mortgage broker has access to over thirty lenders in Canada, giving you the greatest number of choices with the least amount of effort. Only your mortgage broker can speak openly to you about what every lender has to offer. The number one goal is to put you into a mortgage that best suits your individual needs. Which lender you are placed with is of secondary importance.

What about a mortgage broker's educational requirements and qualifications? Each province regulates mortgage brokers through its respective Ministry of Finance. In Ontario, for example, the Financial Services Commission of Ontario (an arm's-length agency of the Ministry of Finance) has set a high standard of education and experience for members practicing in the industry. In addition, mortgage brokers have organized in a few provinces, including British Columbia, Alberta, and Ontario, to establish their own industry associations that also set high standards for their members.

Many mortgage brokers today have earned accounting designations, MBAs, and degrees with economic and financial backgrounds. A specific designation is not essential, but a good mortgage broker (or any mortgage originator, for that matter) should have some qualifications beyond just sales training and experience. You will find most mortgage brokers today far exceed the qualifications of any other representative in any other distribution channel. Below is a list of provincial associations:

- Alberta Mortgage Brokers Association (AMBA)
- Mortgage Brokers Association of BC (MBABC)
- Independent Mortgage Brokers Association of Ontario (IMBA)

As a consumer, it's important to know how the system works and what your options are if you want to make an educated decision. As mentioned, it comes down to the kind of consumer you are. As a mortgage broker, I see all types of clients. Some have more time than others to research their options, but they all have one thing in common: they want to save money. Whichever route you take, the banks will be there to lend you money.

CHAPTER 3

ALL THAT JARGON

It's easy for a mortgage broker to get caught up with all the jargon when speaking with clients about mortgages. Unfortunately, highly educated and well-trained brokers risk sounding bigheaded and can quickly lose their clients' interest if they don't speak to them on a level they can understand. Of course, the industry hasn't helped any by perpetuating so many acronyms and other legalese. I'm sure many wonder if the industry abandoned plain English on purpose as a way to keep clients in the dark. It almost seems like a broker's full-time job is to keep up with mortgage vernacular.

The trouble is that mortgage brokers speak to the lending community all day long, but at any given time, they need to adjust their language when speaking to clients. Perhaps one of the best examples of this is reading a client's credit report. Very few consumers ever request their own report, even though it's free via snail mail. If they do, however, the report they receive scarcely resembles the version of the report the lender or mortgage broker receives. The credit agencies know that very few people could ever understand the broker/lender's version. Although the information is the same, the client's version is written in a narrative format using plain English.

I have often thought consumers should be schooled at an early age about the importance of credit before entering the working world. Sadly, no such programs exist in our secondary schools. This goes double for anyone who receives student loans for post-secondary education. Once you enter the working world, finding the time to take a course on credit management, if one exists, is far less likely. Most of the time, the people who end up taking a class on credit counselling are either in the process of or facing the strong likelihood of bankruptcy. This is definitely the wrong time to get educated.

If you are going to enter the financial waters of homeownership, you had better familiarize yourself with some of the language. I will keep to the basic terms you really need to know.

AMORTIZATION AND TERM

There are two types of terms applied to your mortgage and you need to understand the difference between them. They are not the same, but people tend to use the word *term* interchangeably. The *amortization term* is the amount of time over which your loan is scheduled to be fully repaid. Mortgages traditionally come with a 25-year amortization. At the end of the amortization term, your balance owing is $0. You will have paid back the principal borrowed plus the interest. Today, since house prices are at an all-time high, banks have allowed up to 40-year amortizations to make mortgage payments more affordable.

The other term you will decide on is your *interest rate term*. Whether you go with a fixed-rate or variable-rate mortgage, mortgage interest rates come with a term. For example, if you take a 5-year fixed rate at 4%, the bank will not change the interest rate charged on your mortgage for the next five years. At the end of the five years, your mortgage comes up for renewal and you will decide again on a new interest rate term. Maybe the second time you will decide to take a 10-year term. The rate you get then will be whatever the 10-year rate is at the time of your renewal. That is, five years after your mortgage started. In this example, after completing your two interest rate terms, you are fifteen years into the amortization of your mortgage. If you decided on a 25-year amortization, you now have only ten years to go.

Can you pick an interest rate term to match the amortization term? Yes, this is called a fully amortized loan. The longest interest rate term is twenty-five years, so you are limited to a 25-year amortization. You could also shorten your amortization to ten or fifteen years to match a 10- or 15-year interest rate term, but keep in mind the mortgage payment goes up when you shorten the amortization.

FIXED-RATE MORTGAGE VS. VARIABLE-RATE MORTGAGE

We already discussed the fixed-rate mortgage (FRM) in the last section, but what about the variable-rate mortgage (VRM), also referred to as an adjustable-rate mortgage (ARM)? These interest rates also come with a term, traditionally five years. The pervasive forces of competition, however, have banks now offering them for 1-, 3-, and 5-year terms.

As the name suggests, the interest rate can change over the term. The traditional practice with VRM rates is to tie them to the *prime lending rate*. During the heady days of 2007, VRM rates were discounted as low as prime minus 1%. After the subprime market crash in 2007-2008, banks adjusted their VRM pricing to prime plus 1%. We had a good run of VRM mortgages priced below prime, and it was difficult getting used to saying prime *plus* anything. The good news was even though VRM pricing went north of prime, the prime rate itself dropped to an all time low of 2.25% (May 26, 2010). Eventually the credit markets found their footing and VRM mortgages returned to prime minus a discount.

You might be asking, "What is the prime lending rate and how is it determined?" In late 2000, the Bank of Canada adopted a system of eight preset dates per year on which it announces its *key policy rate*. The bank carries out monetary policy by influencing short-term interest rates. It does this by raising and lowering the *target for the overnight rate*. The overnight rate is the interest rate at which major financial institutions borrow and lend one-day (or "overnight") funds among themselves; the Bank of Canada sets a target level for that rate. This target for the overnight rate is often referred to as the Bank of Canada's *key interest rate* or *key policy rate.*

The expected response by the commercial banks is to adjust or not adjust their commercial *prime lending rate* accordingly. Commercial banks use the prime lending rate as a base to calculate other interest rates they provide, such as a VRM.

INTEREST RATES

The most popular subject when talking about mortgages is interest rates. Getting a good rate can make a big difference in your total interest cost. For example, with a few of the more competitive lenders, I can currently get 1.90% off the banks' posted 5-year rates. On a $100,000 loan, that represents a saving of $9,500. Since you pay your mortgage with after-tax dollars, you can gross up those savings. For example, if you are in the 40% tax bracket, the $9,500 saved is equivalent to getting a $15,833 bonus at work over the same 5-year period.

You should know a few additional things about interest rates. Every lender will hold a rate for a set time while you look to buy a home. This comes with getting a *pre-approval*. Some lenders will hold rates for only sixty days. That means if you buy a house and set the closing date for seventy days later, the lender will not have to honour the rate. If you need more time, rate holds of up to 120 days are available.

Another potential pitfall is the lender's rate drop policy. Between your approval date and the closing date, will you benefit if the rate drops? If so, are there any restrictions? When will the final rate be set?

Finally, how the interest rate is calculated is something everyone should know about. With a few exceptions, Canadian mortgage interest rates are calculated semi-annually. What does that mean? All you need to know is that the more often interest is calculated during a year, the more expensive the loan. There is no connection between how often the interest is calculated and how often you make payments. Insist on having this information fully disclosed. It's the law.

BLENDED-RATE MORTGAGE

You may want or need to increase the amount of your present mortgage in the middle of a term. One option would be to pay the penalty, discharge your existing mortgage, and register the new bigger mortgage at current market rates. Another option would be to acquire a blended-rate mortgage. With this option, your existing contract interest rate and mortgage balance are blended with today's interest rate (on the new term selected) and the new money requested.

Some banks restrict your new term to the remaining term on your existing mortgage. Other banks will allow you to pick a whole new term. This is referred to as *blend and extend*. Some banks, however, won't offer any blending option whatsoever. Make sure you know your bank's policy in advance.

Let's look at an example to see how this translates into numbers. John Smith calls his favourite mortgage broker and says he wants an additional $40,000 to install a pool in his backyard. Three years ago, John took out a mortgage with a 5-year term at 5.49%. He has two years remaining on his current term and the outstanding balance is roughly $298,000.

The bank holding his current mortgage won't do an extend and blend. They will only blend his rate for the remaining two years left on his current mortgage term. If John stays with his current lender and refinances to acquire the additional $40,000, they will waive the penalty to break his current mortgage. However, John must accept the blended rate. The following table is a calculation of John's blended rate:

Blended Rate Calculation

Mortgage wanted	$339,000
Less: Existing mortgage	$298,000
Equals: New money	$41,000
Current (contracted) mortgage rate	5.49%
Remaining term (in months)	24
New mortgage rate	3.60%
New mortgage term (in months)	24
Blended rate	5.26%

In this example, the blended rate is only marginally better that the contract rate John had. That is because the 5.49% contract rate is weighted in the calculation by the much larger $298,000 loan amount. The 3.60% new rate is weighted in the calculation by the smaller $41,000 new money.

By the way, in case you were wondering, I added the additional $1,000 to the $40,000 needed for the pool to cover closing costs. The other variable that factors into the blended rate is the additional time added to the original mortgage term. In this case, no new time was added since John's bank would not blend and extend.

Let's examine the same scenario but with John's bank being willing to blend and extend. If John decided to take a new 5-year term, the additional time would be three years (five years less the remaining two years). In this case, John would be blending his 5.49% contract rate with his bank's new 5-year rate of 3.89%. With the added time factored in, John's blended rate would be 4.45%. See the table below:

Blended-and-Extend Rate Calculation

Mortgage wanted	$339,000
Less: Existing mortgage	$298,000
Equals: New money	$41,000
Current (contracted) mortgage rate	5.49%
Remaining term (in months)	24
New mortgage rate	3.89%
New mortgage term (in months)	60
Blended rate	4.45%

Incidentally, the penalty to break John's mortgage would be $11,264. John might be thinking this is not so bad. Even in the first blended-rate option, he gets a slightly better rate (5.26%) for the remaining two years on his mortgage and the additional cash he wanted to install the new pool without having to pay the penalty. The blend-and-extend option is even better. Make sure you know what you are getting up front.

Another option for John worth mentioning would be leaving his first mortgage alone and adding a second mortgage/line of credit if he had enough equity in his home. A line of credit can be obtained at prime, which at the time of writing is 3%. Would you rather finance the $41,000 at 3% or 4.45%? The restriction for a line of credit, however, is that it cannot exceed 80% of the property's value. To mortgage another $41,000 against the house as a line of credit, John's property would need to have an appraised value of $423,750.

When should you consider a blended rate as an option? You may be interested in refinancing or an equity take-out to consolidate debts, do a home improvement, pay for your child's university education, or perhaps you wish to seek a larger mortgage to be able to purchase a new house. In the latter case, your mortgage would also need to be *portable*. In all cases, not having to pay a penalty to break your mortgage is the key benefit of a blended-rate mortgage.

If your contract interest rate is low compared to the current rates, your blended-rate may still be lower than the current rates. If your contract interest rate is higher than the current interest rates, it could be worth breaking your mortgage and obtaining a new bigger mortgage at the better rates. Ask your mortgage broker to crunch the numbers.

EARLY RENEWAL

Most lenders will allow you to break your mortgage contract and renew early. For example, if you signed a 5-year FRM and midway through decided that interest rates had bottomed out and all indications are that rates will be going up, you may opt to renew early to get the low interest rates for a new term. Unless your bank has a blended-rate mortgage option, you will have to pay the bank a penalty for breaking your mortgage contract. In spite of the penalty, this could still save you money.

PORTABILITY

Portability is a mortgage option that allows you to move to another property without losing your current contracted interest rate. You can keep your existing mortgage balance, term, and interest rate, plus save money by avoiding early discharge penalties.

If you need a bigger mortgage, the bank may let you use portability and then "blend" your interest rate on the extra amount needed. This gives you the mortgage amount you need at a rate that combines both the old and new rates. Most regular mortgages are portable. If, however, your mortgage is classified as a collateral mortgage, it would not likely be portable, as it comes with different charge terms.

The charge term that would disqualify your mortgage from being portable is if the collateral mortgage was "readvanceable."

This charge term, or feature, is characteristic of how a line of credit works. You can pay it down and then run it up again or "readvance" the loan again. The problem with this feature and portability comes with the potential for a loan to exceed the 80% loan-to-value (LTV) threshold. Collateral loans, which are readvanceable, cannot exceed 80% of the property's market value (LTV). For example, if the homeowners are downsizing to a property they purchased for $300,000, but their collateral mortgage is readvanceable to $290,000, this potential LTV exceeds 80%. Even if the outstanding balance on their mortgage is $200,000, the homeowners could potentially increase the loan beyond the acceptable 80% LTV. In this case, $240,000 represents 80% of the property's $300,000 purchase price.

The only other restriction on portability is the property itself. If you are moving to a property the lender will not secure against, portability is not an option. Examples include property with different title covenants, such as a life lease, a co-op, or a mobile property on leased land.

ASSUMABILITY

In Ontario, you have the option to pass your mortgage over to the person buying your home. In the early '80s, when interest rates spiked to an all-time high of almost 22%, this was a popular idea to help sell your home. If you had time remaining on your mortgage (e.g., two years) at 11% when the current rates being offered was at 20%, passing this mortgage to potential buyers could help close the deal. The person buying your home would take over, or "assume," your mortgage. The lender holding the mortgage still has to approve the buyer's creditworthiness, but most lenders offer the feature of assumability.

There is one caveat: in Ontario, if the homebuyer taking over your mortgage defaults, the lender still has recourse to you, the original mortgagor, for payment. This is the reason why assumable mortgages are not common in Ontario. In western Canada, on the other hand, lenders don't have recourse to the original homeowner under default proceedings, making the practice of assuming mortgages more acceptable. Similarly, in the Maritimes, assumability is governed by the mortgage. There are no regulated standard charge terms like in Ontario. In Quebec, the situation appears to be more convoluted. I asked Pierre-Denis Leroux, a practicing lawyer in Quebec with expertise in real estate law, to explain. Below is his response:

> In Quebec, a mortgage doesn't provide the mortgagee a personal recourse against the owner. All it does is provide a recourse against the charged property, be it movable (personal) or immovable (real property), corporeal or incorporeal. This recourse is a right *in rem*. The mortgagee's recourse results from the covenant, which is secured by the mortgage. Such a covenant provides the lender with a recourse *in personam* against the covenantor and may be persued against all properties of the covenantor, which the creditor may seize and have sold in justice to be paid of its claim out of the proceeds.
>
> The proceeds are, as a rule, distributed *pari passu* among the creditors of the covenantor, except for those having a legal cause of preference (hypothecs and prior claims), which rank by preference on the proceeds charged in their favour. Exceptionally, the creditor and the debtor may agree that in the event of a default, the creditor will have the right to pursue execution only against certain assets of the debtor. Most of the time, these assets would be the ones charged in favour of the creditor. This is what we call limited recourse obligations.
>
> When a mortgage loan is assumed in this province in the

context of a sale, it generally means that the mortgage creditor will still benefit on its mortgage on the charged property and that the purchaser has made his own the personal obligations of the vendor (i.e., that he too can now be sued by the creditor in the event of a default). Normally, mortgage loans are assumed on a joint and several basis and the original co-venantor is not released. It is possible for the creditor to release the original borrower. An express release is required for that and the creditor needs to be very careful. The Civil Code of Quebec provides that in such a case, the existing indebtedness is novated and, as a result, the hypothecs initially securing the indebtedness are extinguished, unless a very carefull procedure is followed to reserve them.

As a rule, mortgage lenders refuse to release original borrowers under a mortgage loan. Some institutional lenders would do it, even on the larger loans, but it is quite touchy.

RATE HOLDS

A problem most mortgage borrowers face at some point is the long lead time before a mortgage interest rate can be set. For homeowners patiently awaiting the end of a long term of unstable interest rates, the wait can seem endless. Most lenders won't guarantee any rate until thirty days before the renewal date. For homebuyers, particularly first-timers using long closing periods to save money, the wait can be quite nerve-wracking. The situation could become dangerous if rates jump and they then have to re-qualify at the higher rates.

Some are fortunate enough to have a long-term rate cap available through a builder's financing package. However, most don't have this kind of protection, especially if the purchase is a resale property and the closing exceeds ninety days. Fortunately, you can hedge both situations quite comfortably. While some lenders have been reducing their rate holds, a few have increased theirs from 90 to 120 days.

Here's how it works: Suppose your mortgage matures in four months and you're hoping to renew at a good 5-year rate. By choosing a lender who provides 120 days of rate protection, you can secure the 5-year rate you want today. Similarly, homebuyers who need the extra time to shop and/or save can also benefit from the 120-day rate hold.

In both cases, if rates drop between now and your renewal/closing date, you will get the lower rate. With a rate hold, you will be protected four months in advance in case rates go up.

Very few lenders offer 120-day rate protection. If this is a priority for you, make sure you inform your broker to ensure the selection of an appropriate lender.

RATE DROP POLICY

While it's true that you will get a lower rate if rates go down between now and your renewal/closing date, there is another potential pitfall: the lender's rate drop policy. You need to know the answer to the following questions:

1. When will the final rate be set?
2. How many times can you reset the rate?

If rates have dropped since you were approved, most lenders like to set the rate five to seven days before your renewal/closing date. If there are any further rate drops during this time, too bad. Some lenders will restrict you to one or two rate resets. Even worse, they will require proof in writing that you requested the new lower rate. Just make sure your crystal ball is working so you know when to make the request.

The most dangerous scenario, however, is when rates are unstable: up and down. For example, let's say you are approved at 5% and waiting 120 days for your closing. During that time, rates drop to a low of 4% but come back up to 4.5% just before your closing date. Unless you or your mortgage broker made the request at 4%, the lender will set your final rate at 4.5%.

Fortunately, there are lenders with rate drop policies that avoid all these concerns. That is, with the 120-day rate protection, your final rate will be set right up to and including your renewal/closing date. The lender will do a "look back" to your approval date to see what the lowest rate was during your wait. They will automatically give you the lowest rate during that time—no written request required. Even better, if you change your mind and want to go with a different interest rate term, you also will get the lowest rate for that new term.

BRIDGE LOAN

If you are a first time homebuyer, you needn't worry about bridge loans. If you are buying and selling a home, however, you may need a bridge loan depending on your circumstances. If you are selling a home, you most likely will use the equity in your home as a down payment towards your new home. However, if the closing date on your old home comes after the closing date on your new home, you won't have access to this equity and therefore won't have a down payment to close the purchase on your new home. That's where a bridge loan comes in. It takes care of your down payment until the sale of your old house closes. It doesn't tend to get much more complicated than that. People tend to think it's expensive, but it usually isn't.

Let's take a typical example: Mr. and Mrs. Jones have purchased their second home. They also sold their existing home and will walk away with $50,000 to use as a down payment on their new home. However, since the sale of their existing home closes two weeks after the closing date on their new home, they will need a bridge loan. They already put down $5,000 with their offer (their deposit) on the new home, so they need a bridge loan for the remaining $45,000 for the two weeks following their closing date. They will then receive the $50,000 net proceed from the sale of their old home and pay back the $45,000 bridge loan plus interest.

Most lenders charge around $300 as a setup fee for a bridge loan. The interest rate is usually prime plus 3%. Assuming a current prime rate of 2.75%, prime plus 3% equals 5.75%. Let's do the math:

$$\$45,000 \text{ X } 5.75\% = \$2,587.50 \text{ per year}$$

Therefore:

$$\$2,587.50 / 365 \text{ days} = \$7.09 \text{ per day}$$

Therefore:

$$\$7.09 \text{ X } 14 \text{ days} = \$99.26$$

Therefore, the interest charged on the bridge loan for two weeks is $99.26. This isn't even a third the cost of the setup fee.

Many people who understand the nominal cost of bridge financing ahead of time will purposely use it to avoid having to move twice in one day. The biggest benefit of all is being able to work on the new home without all the furniture and other belongings in the way. Painting and cleaning are much more fun with empty rooms.

Be aware that bridge financing can get expensive. Though you should expect interest charges to rise the bigger the loan amount, the more significant factor is the added legal cost you will incur if you exceed certain limits. If your bridge loan is for less than thirty days and less than $100,000, most banks won't require any collateral. Beyond these thresholds, however, the lender will want to take your old home as collateral. This means your lawyer will now have to do title searches on your old home and register a mortgage for the bridge loan. This is in addition to the same legal work required on your new home, which essentially doubles your legal costs. This could be a rather regressive step compared to paying your mortgage down quickly on your first home and acquiring all that equity.

It's important to note that unless you have two firm offers to purchase (your new home and your old home), you can't even apply for a bridge loan. Your lender needs to know how much you need and for how long you need it. Without the two offers, they can't know either. Remember this if you decide to buy before you sell and go to waive all your conditions.

CONVENTIONAL MORTGAGE

A conventional mortgage is one that doesn't exceed 80% of the purchase price or appraised value (the lesser of the two) of the property (home or investment). The biggest advantage of having a conventional mortgage is avoiding the cost of default insurance, which is required by law under the *Bank Act* if your financing exceeds 80%.

If your conventional mortgage is well below the 80% threshold, you still have room to add a secured line of credit up to the 80% threshold. If your situation is deemed higher risk by the bank, they may limit their financing to a conventional mortgage at 80% LTV, or perhaps even less. For example, many lenders offer "equity programs" to self-employed individuals who cannot prove their income on paper but have good credit. Under the equity program, the lender will relax on traditional income documentation but will limit the mortgage amount to under 80% LTV, or conventional.

HIGH-RATIO MORTGAGE

If you don't have 20% of the lesser of the purchase price or appraised value of the property, your mortgage must be insured against payment default by one of the mortgage insurers—Canada Mortgage and Housing Corporation (CMHC), for example. That means your

LTV ratio is above the 80% threshold. You have crossed the threshold into the high-ratio territory, or higher-risk territory. The one-time cost of the default insurance is typically added to the mortgage amount. Similar to a progressive tax, the insurance premium increases as the amount of risk increases associated with a lower down payment.

Keep in mind this law doesn't apply to all lenders. It depends on what legislation regulates the lender. For example, subprime lenders regulated under the *Mortgage Brokerages, Lenders and Administrators Act* aren't required to insure loans above 80%.

APPRAISAL

Appraisal is the process of determining the value of property, usually for lending purposes. This value may or may not be the same as the purchase price of the home.

If you are interested in buying a rural property, pay close attention to the previous sentence. The problem is that every lender wants their appraised value based on the house plus five acres. With the exception of detached garages, lenders aren't interested in any value associated with other buildings on the property.

Now think about what that could mean in terms of the financing you want. For example, let's say you're interested in purchasing a small hobby farm with two horse stables, a riding ring, and ten acres. This could be worth every penny the vendor is asking at $1 million; however, this type of property doesn't represent a big market with many potential buyers. Lenders will therefore use these parameters to reduce their risk. The appraised value based on the house and only five acres might only be $800,000. If you were looking to finance 95%, it will be 95% of $800,000, regardless of how much higher the sale price is. You will have to make up the difference on your own. No lender, private or institutional, will consider any other value except the appraised value, and 95% financing is as good as it gets.

Cash back mortgages were originally popular only during the busy spring market, but they have become a mainstay available all year long. To the unsuspecting homebuyer, a cash rebate of 3% to 5% of the loan value can be quite tempting. However, a closer look at this marketing ploy reveals substantial money forfeited.

If you elect to take the 3% re(bait), you forfeit any discount on the mortgage rate. Taking the posted rate makes for simple comparisons. For example, if you take a $100,000 5-year mortgage at a current posted rate of 5.79%, you get a 3% cash back of $3,000. Alternatively, you could take the same $100,000 5-year mortgage at the discounted rate of 4.09% and save approximately $8,500 in after-tax dollars. You decide! Even at the 5% cash back ($5,000), you still save approximately $3,500 in after-tax dollars.

Equally important is the size of the mortgage for which you qualify. Assuming you don't need the cash back to cover your closing costs, you have a $60,000 annual household income, $2,000 in property taxes, $100 in monthly heating costs, no other debts, and a 20% down payment, you would qualify for a $212,000 mortgage at the 5.79% posted rate. However, if you went with the discounted rate of 4.09%, you would qualify for a $251,000 mortgage. This can make a big difference in the home you choose to buy.

There is also the clawback associated with most cash back mortgages. That is, if you don't stay put for the duration of your minimum 3- or 5-year term, you must give back the prorated amount of the rebate. In some cases, you must give back the whole rebate.

So, who benefits from the cash back mortgage? If you're like most people, raising the funds for a down payment and closing costs is the hardest part of buying a home. Lenders design this program to assist you with that. However, if you already have these costs covered, look elsewhere to find greater value in your mortgage.

The interest adjustment date (IAD) is the day your mortgage effectively begins to run. Not understanding how they work can devastate your carefully planned cash flow on closing day.

Most lenders like to keep things simple when amortizing your mortgage. They like to begin your payback schedule on the first of the month and receive your payments on the first of the month one month later. However, closing dates can occur every day of the month. To achieve what they want, lenders use the IAD. For example, if you close on September 10, the lender will interest adjust to October 1, your effective starting date, and your first monthly payment will be November 1, covering the interest for the month of October. As for September, you are still responsible for paying interest from the time you received the loan to the IAD—in this case, twenty-one days (September 10 to October 1). The question is, how does the lender collect it?

Much to the displeasure of borrowers, most lenders deduct the twenty-one days of interest from the mortgage advance. Not only that, they also calculate the interest daily, making the charge even more expensive. In our example, if we assume a $200,000 mortgage at 5.79%, the twenty-one days of interest will cost $666.25.

$$\$200{,}000 \times 5.79\% \,/\, 365 \text{ days} \times 21 \text{ days} = \$666.25$$

Therefore, to close the purchase, you will need an extra $666.25. This isn't the kind of surprise you want when you're sitting in your lawyer's office, waiting to close the deal. Closing even earlier in the month— say, September 5—would only compound your cash flow problem.

How can you avoid this potential cash flow killer? The easiest way is to set your closing date for the first of the month, assuming the first of the month is not a Saturday, Sunday, or statutory holiday (all days the land registry office is closed). That eliminates the need for any interest adjustment. Alternatively, if you want to make your mortgage payments weekly or biweekly, you could set your IAD to the day of the week on which you want to make your payments. Most lenders will allow you to schedule your mortgage payments on any day of the week. For example, if your purchase closes on a Tuesday and you want your mortgage payments to be on a Friday, you can set the IAD for the Friday following your Tuesday closing. This shortens your IAD holdback to three days.

Not all lenders use IADs. Some (but too few) will make a full mortgage advance on your date of closing. Others are more flexible with the use of an IAD. Just make sure to discuss the cash flow consequences with your mortgage broker when choosing a closing date and lender. It's difficult enough on your part to raise the money for a down payment and to cover closing costs; you don't need any last-minute surprises. Make sure you are well aware of your options and that you account for all costs.

SECOND MORTGAGES

Having a second mortgage put against your property means you have pledged your property as collateral a second time. You now have two loans, each secured against the same asset: your property. The first mortgage has priority over the second simply because it was registered first. Moreover, if you pledge your property a third time for another loan, it's considered a third mortgage, and so on.

From the lender's perspective, to hold the first mortgage is the most advantageous. It means that when you sell the property, the proceeds from the sale go to pay off the first mortgage, then the second mortgage, and then the third mortgage. Any remaining equity goes to the property owner. To offset the additional risk, the lenders holding subordinate mortgages (mortgages two, three, etc.) will charge a higher rate of interest. The actual rate depends on the borrower's equity in the property, their strength as borrowers, the property's marketability, etc.—the usual stuff.

So, why do people have a phobia about second mortgages? Instead of the number of mortgages, people should be concerned about the amount of money borrowed and their equity position behind it.

The reasons for considering a second mortgage can vary. If you wish to buy a house and are just shy of putting down 20%, you may consider using a second mortgage to avoid paying the expensive default insurance. As a rule, this strategy can make sense if you are borrowing under 85% of the property's value. However, over the last few years, default insurance premiums have continued to drop.

A more typical application for arranging a second mortgage is for debt consolidation or home improvements. To avoid breaking your first mortgage and paying a big penalty, you can arrange a second mortgage. If the purpose of the second mortgage is to consolidate debts, your main concern is cash flow. A second mortgage will often improve your cash flow.

Let's take a closer look at debt consolidation as an example, since it's the most common reason why people arrange a second mortgage. John Smith has the following financial profile:

Property Value $200,000
Gross Monthly Income $4,417

Liability	Monthly Payment	Total Debt
First Mortgage	$1,150	$150,000
Car Loan	$550	$10,000
Consumer Loan	$300	$5,000
Credit Cards	$450	$15,000
Total	$2,450	$180,000

John's monthly debt load ($2,450) is dangerously high at 55% of his income ($2,450 / $4,417). This doesn't even include his utilities, food, entertainment, etc. He could arrange a $30,000 second mortgage to consolidate or pay off his car loan, consumer loan, and credit cards. His new profile would look like this:

Liability	Monthly Payment	Total Debt
First Mortgage	$1,150	$150,000
Second Mortgage	$294	$30,000
Total	$1,444	$180,000

With the same amount of debt as before ($180,000), John has freed up $1,006 per month ($2,450 - $1,444) to pay his debt down faster. The cost of arranging the second mortgage is approximately equal to his one month's savings, and now his debt load is only 33% of his income ($1,444 / $4,417).

Notice John's total debt is 90% of the property's value ($180,000 / $200,000), which is called the loan-to-value (LTV) ratio. Don't run to the bank looking for a second mortgage at 90% LTV. They can only go up to 80%. However, subject to the right qualifications, your mortgage broker should be able to use a private source to fund the second mortgage. To a lesser degree, some institutional lenders will participate in arranging an insured second mortgage, but you will be subject to the high cost of default insurance.

The other option you have is to redo your first mortgage. If your penalty to break isn't too severe (e.g., three months' interest) or, even better, if you are coming up to renewal (there is no penalty on your renewal date), you can pay off your existing first mortgage with a new bigger first mortgage. Most banks and default insurance providers will participate in refinancing your new first mortgage up to 85% LTV. Moreover, if you previously paid the default insurance on your existing mortgage, you only have to pay it again on the new money raised.

The trade-off is you will have to keep your amortization where it is. If you want to refinance your first mortgage and start over with a 25-year amortization again, you will have to pay the default insurance on the full amount of the loan. CHMC calls this a "full premium" refinance, and they will give you a break (refund) if you are refinancing less than two years after an earlier "full premium" refinance as follows:

- 100% refund – less than six months later
- 50% refund – between six and twelve months later
- 25% refund – between twelve and twenty-four months later

The same refunds above apply if you purchase within two years after your last high-ratio purchase.

If you are seeking funds to renovate your home, a second mortgage/line of credit is the preferred way to go. You are again limited to the bank's 80% LTV, so you need to have established lots of equity. For a secured line of credit, the typical interest rate at the time of this writing is prime plus 1%. For a premium, some lenders will go up to 85% LTV. The rate will depend on your credit.

Second mortgages or refinancing your first mortgage can be a useful strategy for consolidating debts and paying it down faster. Where you need to be careful is obtaining the necessary mortgage terms to achieve your payment plans. You *must also* have the discipline to not run up your debts again.

CHAPTER 4
THE LONG AND THE SHORT OF IT

Earlier we covered interest rate terms. Determining which interest rate term to take, fixed or variable, also requires a decision on how long to commit to a term. Should you lock in for a long 5-, 10-, 15-, or 25-year term, or should you take a short 1-, 2-, or 3-year term? Everyone struggles with this question. Determining whether to go fixed or variable is equally difficult, but it's always finding its way into the conversation. What are the right answers?

Under normal circumstances, short-term rates are lower than long-term rates. This means you pay a premium for the security of knowing your interest rate won't change for a longer term. Most people, especially first-time buyers, opt for the security of a long-term mortgage. The most popular choice is a 5-year FRM.

More recently (2008-2009), the relationship between short- and long-term interest rates has been just the opposite: short-term rates have been higher than long-term rates. This is called an inverted yield curve. It sounds a bit academic, but an inverted yield curve has indicated a worsening economic situation five out of six times since 1970. Long-term investors will therefore settle for lower yields now if they think the economy will slow or even decline in the future. We can attribute such a poor economic forecast to the 2008 subprime mortgage market crash and subsequent credit crunch. Do you remember all that tax money the U.S. federal government used to bail out banks? Nevertheless, let's not digress too far. This isn't a book on economics.

When I am asked the questions about whether to go short or long term, FRM or VRM, which is almost every time, I will give my standard answer: There is no right answer. It depends on a few things. First, it depends on your own personal circumstances. Are you planning to live in the house for a long time? Is this your first home or your third and maybe final home? Will your income be changing significantly over the short term? Is someone going on maternity leave or is someone expecting a promotion and perhaps a relocation soon? How much debt do you currently carry? These are some of the questions you should ask yourself.

It also depends on your risk tolerance to interest rate swings. Some people have thicker skin than others. If you are going to lose sleep at night worrying about an increase in interest rates, maybe a VRM is not for you.

There is also historical economic data, which tends to favour a VRM over FRM about 88% of the time. If you are a numbers person and have a low debt-to-income ratio, a medium-to-high risk tolerance, and a desire to stay flexible in your mortgage, then you are a good candidate for a VRM. Independent studies have shown 88% of the time that you will average a better interest rate in a VRM compared to a 5-year FRM. That said, you could be a numbers person but don't want to think about your mortgage for the next five or ten years. In that case, locking into an FRM may be the best solution for you. As I say repeatedly, there is no right answer.

If you're thinking you would prefer an FRM for a long term (five years or longer), consider this added benefit and little-known fact. The danger of locking in for a long term is the associated penalty for getting out of your mortgage should you need to break your mortgage prematurely. Fortunately, there is a statutory right (Section 10 of Canada's *Interest Act*) to break your mortgage with only a three-month interest penalty. The two main conditions for allowing this statutory right are:

1. The mortgage is in an individual's name and not a corporation.
2. The period from signing the original mortgage to its maturity is more than five years, and you want to break the mortgage no sooner than five years plus one day.

The key here is you need to take a term longer than five years. If you go with consecutive 5-year terms, the statutory right will never apply because of lenders' "legal gymnastics." That is, lenders will insert a clause into your mortgage renewal papers, which effectively re-date the mortgage so the renewal date becomes the original date of the mortgage and you never get past the fifth anniversary of your mortgage.

PENALTIES FOR BREAKING YOUR MORTGAGE

Most people fail to think about the penalty for breaking a mortgage until it's too late. If you had good representation when you arranged your mortgage, the subject of early renewals and penalties would have been raised. Why? Well, it may have influenced your decision to go short or long term, FRM or VRM.

With few exceptions, most lenders write the same penalty clause into mortgages. It reads something like this:

Provided there is no default on the mortgage, the borrower has the privilege of renewing this mortgage on any date during the original term on payment of a penalty equal to the greater of the interest rate differential or three (3) months' interest.

Of the two penalties, the interest rate differential (IRD) is more fair and reasonable. It compensates the lender for the lost interest should you have stayed on to the end of your contracted term, and it even factors in the current rates they are left with at the time you break it. More precisely, it's the present value of the difference in the interest rates (contractual vs. current) on the outstanding principal for the balance of the mortgage term.

To understand how IRD and this penalty clause work, let's look at the following example. You borrowed $250,000 to buy a house and took a 5-year FRM at 6%. Your monthly payments amortized over twenty-five years are $1,599.52. Three years later, you have to sell your home and now want to fully pay off the loan. The outstanding balance on your mortgage after three years is $235,663.58. There are two years left on your term and the bank's current 2-year rate is 3.50%.

If the bank were to charge a penalty of three months' interest, you would have to pay a penalty of $3,491.55 (the interest component in payment number thirty-seven of $1,163.85 X 3) to discharge your mortgage. This penalty is at best arbitrary and doesn't reflect the lender's cost to take back the money early and put it back "out on the street."

If the penalty were based on the IRD, a fair penalty reflecting the cost to the bank for taking back the money early would be 2.50% (6.00% - 3.50%) multiplied by $235,663.58 multiplied by two (for the two years remaining on the term) for a total of $11,783.18. But we can't stop there. Since the bank receives this $11,783.18 windfall upfront, it can invest it at 3.50% over the next two years and earn even more interest. That's why to properly calculate the IRD, the *present value* of the difference in the interest rates must be examined, not just the difference in the rates themselves. Thank God for computer programs that can render the present value we are looking for instantaneously. We are looking for the dollar amount that when invested at 3.50% for two years equals $11,783.18. That dollar amount is $10,999.72.

Okay, so we figured out the IRD and it's much more than three months' interest ($10,999.72 > $3,491.55). The bank will therefore charge you the IRD to break your mortgage. However, there are times when the opposite will occur. If lenders have the opportunity to re-lend the money out at a higher interest rate than your contract rate, the IRD penalty would be negative. That is, the bank should pay you for breaking your mortgage. (Like *that* is going to happen.) In such cases, the arbitrary three months' interest prevails. It is worth mentioning, however, that the IRD penalty has the potential to be quite large. I have seen many refinance applications where the IRD penalty was too large to warrant breaking the mortgage.

Now let's get back to what we were really after. How would this penalty clause influence your decision to go short or long term, FRM or VRM? Another thing about penalties: you will recall that you can avoid them by porting your mortgage, having a buyer assume your mortgage, and by blending your interest rate. These are all good strategies, but neither one is 100% reliable as a practical and/or economical alternative. Sometimes your best and only alternative is to break the mortgage. Suffice it to say, you need to address the penalty clause to ensure you will make an informed decision.

There is one last thing about penalties and VRMs that you should know. The IRD is mathematically impossible to calculate on a floating or variable interest rate. Therefore, the only penalty charged on a VRM is the three months' interest penalty. If you felt the VRM was a good fit for you, having this added flexibility to break your mortgage with minimum costs might be the tipping point in deciding between an FRM and VRM. More recently (2010), one lender has allowed you to blend your existing VRM with their current VRM and not pay a penalty. Now that's progress!

CHAPTER 5

THE DIGITAL MOVEMENT

When I started my career in the mortgage industry, we took applications by hand and faxed them to the lender. On a good day, the lender responded via fax with a yes or no within the week. Unbelievably, the old guys in the office would remind us when they had to mail in the applications and wait for the response via Canada Post. Were those the good old days?

Thankfully, the mortgage industry has progressed digitally and progressed quickly. Lenders decided early in the game that they were tired of receiving numerous variations of what a mortgage application should look like. Every mortgage brokerage had its own design: same information but different layout. What's worse, many applications were incomplete and illegible.

With the arrival of mortgage origination software (MOS), a handful of companies quickly staked their territory and licensed their software to brokers and lenders. With the right parameters in place, lenders now would only receive complete and legible applications, and each one looked the same depending on the MOS used.

Similarly, mortgage brokers also received the mortgage commitment letter on the system with the same look regardless of which lender it came back from. A few versions/upgrades later, today's MOS programs have become very efficient for processing mortgage applications with typical same-day turnaround times. Lenders can now underwrite many more applications in much less time. And back office administrative work for mortgage brokers has also greatly improved.

But things haven't slowed down yet. With cloud computing, mortgage brokers today can access their existing client data files, start new applications, submit applications, receive approvals, and order appraisals anywhere they have access to the Internet, thanks to the advent of various wireless and cellular devices accessing secure networks. For an industry that strives to be efficient, productive, and mobile, this is real progress.

At the risk of sounding immodest, when I started my own mortgage brokerage company in 1998, I was one of the first three mortgage brokers across Canada with a website. I had my Yahoo! listing up within twenty-four hours at no cost. I was also one of the first among both brokers and banks to offer an online mortgage application. I took a road less travelled to originate new clients. I did this to differentiate myself, but also because I hated the more traditional methods of pounding the pavement, soliciting different referral sources. I was willing to try something new and not rely completely on the traditional and more competitive avenues.

For me, the Internet was my panacea. It also allowed me to reach out to clients well beyond my geographic boundaries. With my toll-free phone number and e-mail address, I could speak with clients anywhere to conduct mortgage business. Early on in my practice, I would courier or fax documents to clients too far away and impractical to meet. I would go over the documents with them on the phone and they would fax or courier them back depending on the number of documents.

I had one client who lived in Hong Kong. We mortgaged a property they still owned just outside of Newmarket, Ontario, where they once lived. (As per industry regulations, I was restricted to brokering mortgages on Ontario properties only.) I would be on the phone with them at the start of their day, which was typically 11 p.m. for me. When new software came along that allowed me to convert any document I wanted to PDF, I no longer had to use couriers or fax machines. This saved me money, but it also let me put the documents in front of my clients immediately.

Nevertheless, this digital approach to conducting mortgage business isn't for everyone, but it's increasingly becoming the norm. My typical long-distance clients are younger professionals who are technologically savvy and put a premium on their time. I am also able to do my part to gain their trust over the phone and with the efficient manner in which I conduct my business. In my estimation, this is the future of mortgage brokering. I have seen this aspect of my business grow over the years.

Although long-distance clients are a pleasure to do business with, I still always enjoy the opportunity to meet people face to face. This more traditional approach will continue to be my main source of business in the local market. Not surprisingly, however, I also use the digital methods with local clients. They can fill out a secure online application at their convenience and I can send PDFs to them. It's up to them whether they fax or scan and e-mail documents back to me. We usually just get together to sign the mortgage papers.

Recent clients of mine provide a good example of a typical broker/client interaction from beginning to end using today's modern technology. Notice the impact on everyone and that precious commodity we all so desperately want more of: time! Please note that I've changed their names to protect their identities.

John and Jane were move-up homebuyers relocating from Vancouver, British Columbia, to Burlington, Ontario. Like most homebuyers, they turned to the Internet to begin their search for a home. They quickly realized the important first step of being pre-approved for a mortgage. Fortunately for them, they discovered the website MortgageResource.ca, where they could learn all about mortgage finance without the usual bias from any one company or industry representative. They could even interact with mortgage originators across the country and across all distribution channels using the website's social media to see what channel was best for them.

As soon-to-be residents of Burlington, Ontario, John and Jane ended up using the website's link to my secure online mortgage application to apply for a mortgage. The following lists the steps they took to obtain their pre-approved mortgage and subsequently close on a purchase.

1. John and Jane contacted me by e-mail with some of their initial questions and concerns. John was the director of franchise development across Canada for a large restaurant chain and spent a lot of time on the road. He didn't have time to sit down with anyone until late in the day when he could send and receive e-mails. Eventually, our e-mails led to a conversation on the phone to nail down the details of what they wanted in a mortgage.

2. When they were ready to apply, John used my secure online mortgage application, again, at the end of his busy day, a process that would have taken twenty to thirty minutes to complete.

3. I could reach John on his cellphone the next day to button down a few details missing on his application, and then I was ready to submit his application electronically for the product and lender we decided was best suited for them using the mortgage origination software.

4. The lender received my application and within four hours sent John and Jane's pre-approved mortgage (PAM) back to me on the system.

5. It was easy to forward them a copy of their PAM because it was in PDF format. A PAM generally doesn't need to be signed, but

I invited John and Jane to call or e-mail me back with any questions they had about their PAM.

6. With little knowledge of the Burlington area, I was able to provide John and Jane with the names of some real estate agents and lawyers who worked in Burlington to help with their purchase. After a short while, they decided not to buy and instead chose to rent a home until they could learn more about the city and its numerous neighbourhoods.

   About a year later, they called me up to say they were ready. I spent a few minutes on the phone with them to update their application on my system. Once again I had them pre-approved the same day. This time, however, they knew exactly where they wanted to buy.

7. As soon as the offer to purchase was written up, John and Jane's agent e-mailed me a copy along with the MLS property listing. This gave me the property information and closing date needed to complete their application, and I resubmitted their application to the lender.

8. The lender again responded with an approval the same day, subject to the usual conditions. Having had John and Jane pre-approved assured us a quick turnaround from the lender when time was of the essence.

9. We took advantage of Jane being in Burlington to meet face to face to sign the lender's approval, or commitment letter. With other clients who are further way, I often will e-mail a copy of the commitment letter and go through it with them over the phone like I did with John and Jane's PAM.

10. If clients have their employment and down payment documenta-

tion together when we meet to sign the lender's approval, I will collect this from them at that time. Such was the case with John and Jane. Otherwise, this, and any other support documentation for satisfying the conditions of the mortgage, would have to be faxed or scanned and e-mailed to me at a later date. *Important*: if your offer to purchase includes a condition of financing (COF), you usually have three to five banking days to satisfy the condition (always aim to get five days). It's important to make sure the lender has enough time to do their due diligence with the support documentation provided to them. During the busy seasons (spring and fall), lenders will need an extra day or two to handle the extra volume of applications. Therefore, make sure you have discussed with your mortgage broker what documentation is required ahead of time so you don't lose any time.

These conditions should also be spelled out in your PAM. Everyone appreciates a client who is organized. More important, the lender can process your application quicker when all the documentation is provided together rather than piecemeal. The last thing you want to do is remove the COF only to hear back from the lender that your support documentation is not acceptable. This is where you need to pay close attention to the details.

11. Since John and Jane's down payment exceeded 20%, they didn't require default insurance. But that means the lender also required a full appraisal on the property to confirm the property's market value and purchase price were the same. It was my job as their mortgage broker to order the appraisal and have the results in the lender's hands to satisfy the condition before the COF deadline. To do this efficiently and cost effectively, I ordered the appraisal online through a third-party agency.

In the process of ordering the appraisal on the agency's website, I was immediately given a list of appraisers in the subject property's area, and their price, to choose from. Additional information on the list included the distance to the subject property's location from the appraiser's office, the average turnaround time for the appraiser, and a grading or score card of the appraiser, voluntarily provided by other mortgage brokers. Facilitated by the agency's website, the appraiser's report, once completed, was e-mailed directly to the lender's underwriter and to me no later than the deadline I requested when making the order.

12. Digital technology has also improved the process of forwarding support documentation to lenders to satisfy conditions of the loan. More lenders are investing in the broker channel and upgrading their systems to facilitate this process. The trend has been to improve the lender websites so that mortgage brokers can securely log in and upload documents directly to the underwriter. The mortgage broker can attach comments to any document uploaded and a confirmation is recorded on the website that the documents were received.

    A history of all uploaded documents and real-time discussions between mortgage broker and underwriter are recorded. Gone are the days when faxed documents for my clients were put in a pile with other borrowers' documents, waiting to be pulled by the underwriter, or worse, get lost in the shuffle!

13. Once the lender receives the signed commitment and all the conditions are satisfied, official mortgage instructions are sent to the client's lawyer, usually no earlier than two weeks before closing or moving day. Today, most lenders still prefer to send original mortgage instructions via courier.

14. Lenders like to confirm with the mortgage broker by fax or e-mail when all conditions have been met. Even better are the lenders who also confirm the date when mortgage instructions

were sent out to the lawyer. Again, with lenders who have invested more in the broker channel, this information is readily available on their secure website. This is a great tool for confirming all the details of the loan. Even after all the aforementioned confirmation, it's always a good idea in the last two weeks before closing for the mortgage broker to check with the lawyer to make sure that everything is in order.

Mistakes sometimes happen, especially during the busy seasons, and this is your last chance to fix them. For example, clients may have a special request for the interest adjustment date (IAD) to make their scheduled payments fall on the right day in line with their pay week. Moreover, it's often the case that changes in the mortgage terms are introduced after the lender's original commitment letter was issued and signed (i.e., the client decides to put down a bigger down payment or decides to go with a variable rate instead of a fixed rate). No one likes surprises. When the client is sitting down with the lawyer to sign the final paperwork and finish the process, whom do you think they will call if something looks wrong? It's incumbent on the mortgage broker to stay proactive.

Advances in digital technology have greatly improved the efficiency, consistency, accuracy, and reliability of the process. In the end, regardless of geographic distance between broker and client, the process of getting a mortgage put together is much faster and easier—and, it is hoped, less stressful—with the help of today's technological advances.

CHAPTER 6

KEY ADVISORS

This might be the most important chapter you read. As I mentioned earlier, purchasing a home is likely the most money you will ever spend at one time. The process involves working with a few trusted advisors, including a mortgage broker. What you will soon discover is that everyone in the industry has referrals at the ready. Whom they suggest to you, however, may or may not be your best option. Getting a referral from someone you know and trust is a safe bet, but at some point, if not from the beginning, you may be working with people you have just met. Be sure to go in with your eyes open and ask many questions.

Each advisor you work with can refer you to another. Just be sure the advisor does so for the right reasons. Oftentimes, money or gifts will change hands for the referral business. If this is fully disclosed to you above the table, I don't have a problem with it. We can all incur advertising costs to generate new business, but a more reliable method is through recommendations or referrals we receive from our industry associates. This is worth more to me than any form of advertising. Just make sure the person you are dealing with is above board regarding the disclosure of compensation. Again, keep your eyes open and ask many questions.

Almost all of the key advisors you will work with are regulated by government legislation or self-regulatory bodies that have strict full-disclosure requirements. For example, in Ontario, under the *Mortgage Brokerages, Lenders and Administrators Act*, a mortgage broker is required to disclose any referral fees paid to the referring party.

Full disclosure requirements are meant to protect you from making an uninformed decision. Any advisor looking out for your best interest will have nothing to hide and will be 100% compliant with the full-disclosure requirements.

Below are some other items that must be disclosed to you under the *Mortgage Brokerages, Lenders and Administrators Act*. I have reproduced them verbatim as they appear on the Ministry-regulated forms. These are things you might want to know about ahead of time:

1. The Mortgage Broker/Agent has the following relationship which may be a potential conflict of interest:

2. Describe any direct or indirect interest that the Brokerage has or, as currently contemplated, may acquire in the transaction for which this disclosure statement is provided.

3. The Brokerage may receive a bonus or contingent commission from the Lender. Contingent commissions may be based on factors such as the volume of business placed with the Lender, or a certain percentage of growth in the placement of business over a previous period.

4. The Lender involved in this transaction may provide the brokerage fees or incentives dependent on the interest rate and the term(s) accepted by the Borrower. The brokerage may retain the fees and incentives or may use them for the benefit of another of the brokerage's clients.

5. The Brokerage has placed over 50% of their business with
_____ during the previous fiscal year.

Pay particularly close attention to items 4 and 5. Depending on the risk and workload associated with your file, a mortgage broker may be entitled to accept more commission from the lender at the expense of your getting a higher interest rate. This is perfectly acceptable under the right circumstances. However, be wary of mortgage brokers out for their own interests.

As for item 5, assuming this is filled out honestly, any mortgage broker placing a disproportionate amount of business with one lender raises a red flag. It may be apt to be suspicious of this practice, as most lenders will pay mortgage brokers a volume bonus. Just make sure the terms you receive are the best available in the market for your circumstances.

Over the course of buying a home and moving in, you will likely employ the services of the following key advisors:

1. Mortgage broker
2. Real estate agent
3. Lawyer
4. Home inspector
5. Real estate appraiser
6. Builder/contractor
7. Insurance broker

By now, I hope you have a good idea of the benefits of using a mortgage broker. I will not belabour their virtues any more. However, it's no accident that I put them at the top of the list. Without exception, the very first thing you should do is get yourself pre-approved. Whether you own a house already or you are buying your first home, this is the first step you should take. Your mortgage broker is there to do the work for you.

Being pre-approved for a mortgage is a critically important step in the process of buying a home, and I can't give up the opportunity to tell you why. Getting yourself a pre-approved mortgage costs nothing except the time you spend obtaining one, and today it couldn't be more convenient. Without leaving your home, you can call your local mortgage broker (to be sure to get the best mortgage in the market) and within hours, you will have your written commitment from the bank. One added advantage is the protected interest rate of up to 120 days that comes with your pre-approval. That gives you lots of time to shop around and no risk of having to requalify later at a higher interest rate if rates jump. With your pre-approved mortgage, you will know exactly how much you can afford.

If you are selling a home first, your mortgage broker can also determine the net proceeds you will have from the sale of your home after deducting all the applicable costs (e.g., mortgage penalty, legal, realtor, etc.). Whether you are selling a home or not, your mortgage broker can help determine what your maximum down payment will be. Armed with this information—the size of mortgage you can afford and what your down payment will be—you are ready to start looking for a home. Everyone will appreciate your knowledge of what you can afford and your focus on homes in the appropriate price range.

A corollary: Having a pre-approved mortgage will strengthen your bargaining position with the vendor of the home you wish to buy. Look at it from the vendor's perspective. If you had two offers on the table for your home, one from a fully pre-approved buyer and the other from a buyer who hasn't made any effort to get pre-approved, which one would you take more seriously?

A caveat: Even though you took the right steps to be pre-approved, the bank will still need to approve the property you're buying. Therefore, your offer to purchase should still be conditional on financing. Very few properties don't measure up, and the condition can be waived in short order. Nevertheless, you don't want any surprises and be stuck with a house and no mortgage. If you're in heavy competition for a home, you may be asked to consider dropping your condition on financing. If you were already pre-approved, you would be more comfortable making this decision. Just make sure you consult with your mortgage broker about any potential problems the lender may have with the property (e.g., well and septic, no basement, UFFI, asbestos in the siding, etc.).

The following descriptions are based on information provided by CMHC.

REAL ESTATE AGENT

Your real estate agent is likely the next key advisor you will work with once you are pre-approved for a mortgage. No one will play a more important role in helping you find a home than your real estate agent. Your real estate agent's job is to:

- help you find the perfect home;
- write an offer to purchase;
- negotiate on your behalf to get you the best possible deal; and
- provide you with important information about the community, help you arrange and coordinate a home inspection, and essentially save you time, trouble, and money.

When the time comes to select a real estate professional, see if you can get a referral from someone you know and trust who has had experience with the recommended agent. Your mortgage broker can also be a good source. There are even good websites such as GoodRealEstateAgents.com.

Don't be afraid to ask questions, especially about any possible service charges. Vendors normally pay a commission to the agent, but some agents charge buyers a fee for their services.

If you would like to know more about a real estate agent's ethical obligations, you can visit the Canadian Real Estate Association's website at www.crea.ca or call your local real estate association.

LAWYER

You need a lawyer (or a notary in Quebec) to protect your legal interests. This may include ensuring that the property you are thinking of buying doesn't have any building/ statutory liens or charges and/or work or cleanup orders associated with it. A lawyer will review all contracts before you sign them, especially the offer (or agreement) to purchase. Having a lawyer involved in the process will give you peace of mind and ensure that things go as smoothly as possible. Law associations such as the Law Society of Upper Canada can refer you to lawyers who specialize in real estate law. In Quebec, contact the Chambre des notaires du Québec for the names of notaries specializing in real estate law.

Lawyers' fees depend on experience and on the complexity of the transaction. For instance, if you are buying a condominium, you will want a lawyer experienced in condominium transactions. It's always a good idea to shop around for rates. Remember that a lawyer should:

- be a licensed full-time lawyer/notary;
- be local and understand real estate laws, regulations, and restrictions;
- have realistic and acceptable fees;
- be able and willing to explain things in plain language; and
- be experienced with condominiums (if you are purchasing a condominium).

You should consider having any home you are thinking of buying inspected by a knowledgeable and professional inspector regardless of whether it's a resale home or a brand new home.

A home inspection is a visual inspection, and the home inspector's role is to inform you about the property's condition. The inspector will tell you if something isn't functioning properly, needs to be changed, or is unsafe. The inspector will also inform you of repairs that you may need to make and maybe even problems that have occurred in the past.

Every inspection should include a visual assessment of at least the following:

1. Foundation
2. Doors and windows
3. Roof and exterior walls
4. Attics
5. Plumbing and electrical systems (where visible)
6. Heating and air conditioning systems
7. Ceilings, walls, and floors
8. Insulation (where visible)
9. Ventilation
10. Septic tanks, wells, or sewer lines (if the inspector is qualified)
11. Any other buildings such as a detached garage
12. The lot, including drainage away from buildings, slopes, and natural vegetation
13. Overall opinion of structural integrity of the buildings
14. Common areas (in the case of a condominium, strata, or cooperative)

There is presently no mandatory certification and no legislated requirements for home inspectors to take any courses or to pass any examinations. Anyone can claim to be a home inspector. However, a good home and property inspector generally belongs to a provincial or industry association. CMHC doesn't recommend or endorse any individual home inspector or association. CMHC supports national standards of competency for home inspectors. For more information about the home inspection industry's voluntary National Certification Program, visit the website of the Canadian Association of Home & Property Inspectors (CAHPI) at www.cahpi.ca.

Home inspector fees are generally in the $500 range and depend on the size and condition of the home. When choosing a home inspector, it's best not to rely on anyone else involved with your purchase. It's all right to ask your mortgage broker or real estate agent for some reputable names, but it would be best for the home inspector to know you didn't use a referral. The last thing you want is a home inspector influenced by the source of the business. Like most of us in the industry, home inspectors rely a lot on referral business. Keep this in mind.

REAL ESTATE APPRAISER

Having a property independently appraised before you make an offer is a good idea. It will tell you what the property is worth and help ensure that you aren't paying too much. Your lender may also ask for a recognized appraisal before completing a mortgage loan. Just make sure the appraiser you choose is on your lender's approved list of appraisers. Your mortgage broker will see to this.

The appraisal should include an unbiased assessment of the property's physical and functional characteristics, an analysis of recent comparable sales, and an assessment of current market conditions affecting the property. Appraisal fees may vary, but you shouldn't pay more than $200 to $350 in most areas for a typical single-family house.

If your mortgage requires default insurance, you may not need an appraisal, depending on the insurance company used. If the insurance company does require it, they will pay for it. If your loan is conventional and doesn't require the default insurance, you will need an appraisal and the cost is your responsibility. If your conventional mortgage gets lower than 50% LTV, the lender may not require it unless your mortgage application was approved under an equity program wherein you didn't have to prove your income.

BUILDER/CONTRACTOR

If you are planning to construct a home, you will have to hire a builder or contractor. If the house you are buying needs renovations, you may also require a builder or contractor.

Here are some things to keep in mind when choosing a builder or contractor:

- Ask for references and talk to other customers about the builder's performance.
- Check with the New Home Warranty program in the area (if applicable).
- Visit other housing developments that the company has built.
- Ask builders or contractors if they are members of a local home-builders' association or ask for a provincial license number.

If you are having a custom home built, remember that:

- You may want to hire an architect to design the house and supervise construction.
- Builders of custom homes usually work on either a fixed-price or a cost-plus basis. Authorize any changes to your contract by writing your name or initials beside the change.

In general, make sure your contract is as specific as possible about construction details, right down to the brand name or model number of any finishes. Make sure that you initial any changes to your contract.

INSURANCE BROKER

An insurance broker can help you with your insurance needs, including property insurance and mortgage life insurance. Lenders insist on property insurance because your property is their security for your loan. Property insurance covers the replacement cost of your home, so premiums may vary depending on its value.

Your lender may also suggest that you buy mortgage life insurance, which provides coverage for your family if you die before you pay your mortgage off. Remember, mortgage life insurance is optional. Don't let anyone tell you otherwise.

Be careful not to confuse property or life insurance with mortgage default insurance, which may be required for high-ratio mortgages.

CHAPTER 7

INDUSTRY ASSOCIATIONS

The goal of every profession is to be self-regulated. The mortgage industry is no different; however, it hasn't happened yet. When I started my career in 1992, the Ontario Ministry of Finance was the regulatory body, and our industry association was the now defunct Ontario Mortgage Brokers Association (OMBA). On my desk, I still have a paperclip holder I received from OMBA back then during a trade show I attended. Its motto looks up at me every day: "Service with integrity." Unfortunately, OMBA was on its way out shortly after I started my career. My understanding of OMBA at the time was that it fell out of favour with the Ministry. My guess is it probably spent too much time trying to defend members the Ministry was trying to, and eventually did, put out of business.

In 1994, the Canadian Institute for Mortgage Brokers and Lenders (CIMBL) arrived and OMBA expired shortly thereafter. However, CIMBL's mission was to represent all of Canada and all segments of the Canadian mortgage industry, not just mortgage brokers.

The majority of Ontario mortgage brokers eventually became unhappy with the diluted representation by CIMBL, so the Independent Mortgage Brokers Association of Ontario (IMBA) was founded in September 2000 to represent Ontario mortgage brokers exclusively.

Oddly enough, although its mission is to advance the mortgage brokerage industry, it too accepts members from all segments of the mortgage industry. It appears that organizations such as these need to find funds wherever they can in order to succeed.

In 2007, CIMBL reconstituted itself and changed its name to the Canadian Association of Accredited Mortgage Professionals (CAAMP). After launching the first ever designation for mortgage industry professionals—the Accredited Mortgage Professional (AMP)—in 2004, it decided to rebrand the organization and focus on advancing the designation across the industry. Eventually, you couldn't be a member of CAAMP unless you paid your way to obtain and maintain the AMP designation.

IMBA responded soon after, in January 2007, by launching its own designations: the Certified Mortgage Professional Agent (CPMA) and the Certified Professional Mortgage Broker (CPMB). Unlike membership in CAAMP, however, members of IMBA are not required to hold either of the aforementioned designations. The decision to obtain a CPMA or CPMB designation is left to the individual mortgage agent or broker.

If I sound a little cynical, you will have to forgive me. I was a supporting member of CAAMP since the inception of my brokerage company in 1998, but when it was put to the test to uphold its own code of ethics and the importance of a sound industry complaints/discipline process, I was sadly disappointed. I wrote an article on the subject, which was published in the September 2008 issue of *Canadian Mortgage Professional* magazine. For your benefit, below is the article in its entirety:

AMP – Almost a Mortgage Professional
By Blair Anderson

AMP – Almost a Mortgage Professional is how one broker I spoke to last year described the Accredited Mortgage Professional designation. Unfortunately, I can't say a whole lot more about the dubious title. I will admit I was one of the first to jump in and obtain my new accreditation. The idea was creditable and I still support any effort that puts forward the position and professionalism of today's honest working mortgage originator. When put to the test of upholding such lofty standards placed on its members, however, CAAMP dropped the ball.

A long-time member of CAAMP since I started my brokerage in 1998, it was a disappointing experience when the day came that I filed a complaint. In all my years brokering I had never filed a complaint against anyone. Yes I had heard stories about conduct unbecoming a professional, but I had not dealt with it firsthand. And then one day I had two rather unassuming immigrants walk into my office looking for a second opinion on a second mortgage they signed up for.

I couldn't sit on my hands and ignore what I witnessed. One of the more disconcerting facts was that the individual broker involved with these clients held the same CAAMP membership card as me. This was a good opportunity, so I thought, to see how enforceable the organization's Code of Ethics was. So I filed a complaint with CAAMP in accordance with its complaints process. I also suggested the clients file a complaint with the Financial Services Commission of Ontario (FSCO).

In my letter, I cited inappropriate conduct and a violation of rules 1, 2, 3, 5, and 10 of the CAAMP Code of Ethics—the latter being the most serious vis-à-vis the broker's predatory lending practices and outright fraud. I enclosed the broker's Statement of Mortgage as evidence of this charge. The total cost of borrowing was 42.729%, but the broker's disclosure was only 14.878%.

The inappropriate conduct included: making the client wait one month for an answer; not disclosing his fee until the clients came in to sign—a drive from Burlington to North York, no less; not providing the client a copy of the lender's commitment letter; asking the client to sign without dating anything; and telling the client not to contact a lawyer. The broker's high pressure and delay tactics were a throwback to a much earlier period of time when this boiler room practice was more prevalent and far less noticed—not to mention most of this conduct was a breach of the *Ontario Mortgage Brokers Act*.

This is a sad commentary and doesn't speak to the professional image the majority of us have worked hard to establish. I expected CAAMP would act quickly to discipline the accused. And I was more encouraged to file my complaint after reading the CAAMP complaints process, which stated:

> Handling consumer and industry complaints is one of CAAMP's most important functions…. Effective complaint handling ensures CAAMP is able to uphold the high standards both members and consumers expect. CAAMP's complaints process ensures legitimate complaints are appropriately considered, while protecting members from frivolous ones.

Unfortunately, nothing was done—not even a slap on the wrist. And what bothered me the most was CAAMP's handling of my complaint—yet another well-conceived process written into their constitution. It was approaching two years after I officially filed my complaint that I learned of the outcome. To top it all off, CAAMP didn't notify me of the outcome. After several ignored e-mails, I finally received this response:

Your complaint against Mr. X was investigated by Financial Services Commission of Ontario. When their investigation was completed, they confirmed with me that they could not find any evidence that would cause them to take any action against Mr. X and they dismissed the complaint. As a result of FSCO's decision to dismiss the complaint, the Chair of the Ethics committee determined that your complaint would not be referred to a Hearing Committee and the file was closed.

Wow! That's some complaints process. And, yes, I was equally disheartened to hear that FSCO did nothing. CAAMP did make it clear they would be waiting on the FSCO outcome for legal reasons I find it difficult to digest. It seems one only needs to threaten a lawsuit against CAAMP and it will back down. I was told by CAAMP the accused had filed 187 pages of documents in his defence.

I still had hope in the early going when CAAMP communicated to me the following:

> Even if FSCO dismissed the complaint, CAAMP will proceed with your complaint against Mr. X. The Chair and members of a hearing panel looked at the evidence earlier this year and they believe that this case justifies a hearing of the Ethics committee. We are ready to go to a hearing once we get word about FSCO's response.

Was this the same Chair of the Ethics committee? Sadly, no hearing ever happened. In the end, Mr. X bluffed and walked, and our industry took a giant step back. If we are to move forward and truly become a self-regulated profession, we need an industry association that will stand up to talk the talk and fight the fight. I personally don't buy the argument that CAAMP was afraid of getting sued. Furthermore, what message does that send to the membership about its integrity and vigilance? CAAMP's Code of Ethics and complaints process are just fine in writing, but this industry needs far more than hollow words of wisdom. Having a Code of Ethics behind your name or title is one thing, but standing behind your members and enforcing the code is a far greater acclamation.

The good news is, I was able to arrange a second mortgage (line of credit) for my clients with a reputable institutional lender, and at a cost they could agree with.

Needless to say, CAAMP was not happy about the article. However, it wasn't my idea to go public with my discontent. The magazine approached me to write a piece on the industry, good or bad. The timing of their request, unfortunately, was when I was still brewing with contempt. I chose to expose a side of the industry that I felt needed exposing. The magazine was happy with what I wrote, and I did receive praise from my peers who phoned me to say thanks.

The experience left me with a jaded view of any industry association. Although the industry needs them if it ever wants to reach a high level of professionalism and self-regulation, a membership card isn't what makes a good mortgage broker. Remember that!

As indicated earlier, Canada falls a bit short of local representation with only three provincial associations. CAAMP, on the other hand, endeavours to be the national voice of the mortgage industry. Below is the contact information of each organization:

Alberta Mortgage Brokers Association (AMBA)
www.amba.ca   888-452-2652
Mortgage Brokers Association of British Columbia (MBABC)
www.mbabc.ca   877-371-2916
Independent Mortgage Brokers Association of Ontario (IMBA)
www.imba.ca   877-564-4622
Canadian Association of Accredited Mortgage Professionals (CAAMP)
www.caamp.org   877-442-4625

If you look at the mission statements and constitutions of the two provincial associations out west, the message is much the same—for example, "Set uniform standards and establish a code of ethics to govern the members of the association for the protection of the public" is an excerpt taken from MBABC's constitution.

With a healthy membership of over 1,800, MBABC, which incorporated in 1990 as a non-profit organization, appears to be well organized to represent the province's mortgage industry and its membership. They have not followed IMBA in creating their own industry designation; instead, their professional development efforts have been to offer courses that support the AMP designation and its progression.

I read their Ethics Complaint and Committee Process. Just like CAAMP's and IMBA's, it's a well-conceived and well-written protocol. Here's an excerpt, however, that sounded familiar, and not in a good way: "License under review (pending ruling by regulator), no action will take place on the part of MBABC."

In Alberta, AMBA is the collective voice of the province's mortgage industry. Another non-profit, AMBA was founded in 1975 and has a membership of 1,300. According to their website, they promote "an ethical and sustainable industry for consumers and industry members." In addition to offering the mandatory courses for provincial licensing, AMBA offers a number of good courses for continuing education and professional development. Very little is written on the AMBA website regarding a formal complaints procedure. They do have an Ethics Committee, and they will investigate complaints against members who breach the bylaws or code of ethics and who don't provide professional standards of practice.

The day of self-regulation may come, and I truly hope it does. The Canadian mortgage industry is filled with countless examples of advancements in professionalism, technology, and good fiscal management (e.g., the Canada Mortgage Bond). However, with the recent subprime mortgage crisis—a problem largely rooted in the U.S.—and the subsequent broader economic crises, I don't expect much movement in that direction any time soon.

CHAPTER 8

SUPERBROKERAGES

Like most other healthy and competitive industries, the Canadian mortgage brokerage industry has evolved over time. What started out as a vast number of small independent shops with anywhere from one to fifteen brokers now includes a few "superbrokerages" and large national networks, thanks in large part to consolidation. For the sake of this discussion, we define a superbrokerage as a regional or national organization that is very large both in terms of the number of brokers/agents and volume of business.

A relatively young industry with lots of potential for growth, the mortgage brokerage industry has attracted the capital of investors looking to make a bigger splash. It was inevitable that mortgage brokerage companies would eventually unite to establish a regional or national presence, where the typical benefits of branding and economies of scale could be achieved.

Mortgage Intelligence and Invis were two of the early superbrokerages to arrive, in 2000. Roughly eight years later on October 1, 2008, they merged to become the largest superbrokerage in the country with $100 billion in mortgages funded between them by 2010. The merger passed without any press release or media coverage whatsoever. Rumour has it that the low profile was no accident. Years earlier in April 2002, Mortgage Intelligence sold the company to a lender, GMAC Residential Funding of Canada Limited.

Part of the strategy was to give Mortgage Intelligence brokers and agents exclusive rights to mortgage products offered by GMAC. It didn't take too long, however, before GMAC wanted a bigger piece of the pie and opened the doors to do business with other independent mortgage brokers. This didn't go over well with the brokers and agents at Mortgage Intelligence who had given up their independence to be affiliated with a lender no other mortgage broker could work with. I also think GMAC didn't want people to know how much they sold Mortgage Intelligence to Invis for.

Other superbrokerages dotting the landscape include the Mortgage Alliance and the Mortgage Centre. Both companies entered the market before Mortgage Intelligence and Invis. Along with the Mortgage Centre, HLC Home Loans Canada is a division of CIBC Mortgages Inc. And more recently, Dominion Lending Centres entered the marketplace. Each superbrokerage has a different value proposition from the others, but it's the follow-through that will determine which ones will last. With such a mobile labour market, companies had better hold true to what they promise.

The debate continues, however, as to whether the superbrokerage model can best serve the industry. The service provided to you, the consumer, is what matters most. I have my own opinion on the subject, of course, as does everyone else. As a consumer advocate, it's my duty to illuminate the pros and cons from your perspective. You can decide for yourself which model would best serve you. To achieve this, I will attempt to compare both models (superbrokerage vs. small independent) side by side.

I will first discuss superbrokerages from the perspective of the mortgage brokers and agents who might consider working there. It's fair to say that almost all of the advantages of a superbrokerage are for the brokers and agents who work for them. Superbrokerages will claim these include such things as:

1. Branding on a national level
2. Marketing support
3. Ownership opportunities
4. Higher commission splits
5. Volume bonus incentives
6. Training and education
7. Lower operating costs
8. Centralized underwriting and fulfillment
9. Client retention services
10. Payroll and back-office administrative support
11. Legislative compliance services
12. Program/service innovation
13. Lender relationships

The above thirteen points are worthy of any broker's attention but aren't exclusive to superbrokerages. I will address each of the items from the perspective of a small independent brokerage:

(1) *Branding on a national level.* Having the resources to implement regional or national advertising campaigns, or retaining a celebrity corporate spokesperson such as Don Cherry, may raise public awareness about the superbrokeage brand, which can be good for the superbrokerage and its brokers, but it doesn't guarantee better service to the consumer. Small independents believe that being attached to a national brand is not all it's cut out to be. You lose the autonomy to serve your clients the way you want, and if consumers have a bad experience with one broker or franchise within the national brokerage house, the entire chain gets a bad name. Chains are only as good as the weakest link.

It has always been my feeling that a small independent brokerage house, as a company, is only as strong as the community it serves. They therefore put a greater emphasis on supporting the community where they live and work. Investing time and money in community programs, and people, is a better way of establishing a worthy reputation, along with the quality of mortgage broker service provided.

(2) *Marketing support* and (6) *training and education*. Superbrokerages have the resources to implement quality education, training, and market support by virtue of a larger capital base. However, the group dynamic of a small office in a cooperative environment is as effective a support structure as any broker needs. In addition, everyone in a small brokerage discusses and agrees to company decisions about marketing and business development, not just the people who started the company.

(3) *Ownership opportunities*. One of the strategies superbrokerages use to attract brokers is to provide the opportunity to own shares in the company and share the profits. Remember, every superbrokerage has its own value proposition. Some hire brokers with the more traditional "independent contractor agreement." With some superbrokerages, you're actually an employee wherein stock option programs and purchase plans can have serious tax implications. Most small independent brokerages that I know use the traditional independent contractor agreement.

(4) *Higher commission splits,* (5) *volume bonus incentives,* and (7) *lower operating costs*. It's no secret that national brokerage houses qualify for volume bonus incentives offered by the banks by reaching the highest tiers available, while small independents may not even qualify for the lower tiers. Superbrokerages can also offer brokers higher commission splits and cover some of their operating costs, including credit reports, licensing, errors and omissions insurance, and association memberships. So why don't superbrokerages attract everyone?

First, many variables come in to play when looking at commission structures and volume bonuses at superbrokerages. The money paid out depends on several factors: the products sold, the lenders used, whether the broker is part of a franchise, and if the superbrokerage has programs to which the brokers and agents contribute. Suffice it to say, each superbrokerage has a different way in which it splits commissions and volume bonuses based on its value proposition.

For the very same reasons (i.e., products sold and lenders used), it wouldn't make economic sense for all small independents to switch over to a superbrokerage. Some small independents spread their business around more or work more with privates and subprime lenders, who may or may not offer any volume bonuses. Paying royalties to superbrokerages in these cases would end up costing the small independent more money than they would make.

I have always had concerns about the level of business some brokers originate with one lender regarding the incentive to reach volume bonuses, and not to mention the affiliations some superbrokerages have with one lender. Is this conflict of interest less influential for the small independent?

(8) *Centralized underwriting and fulfillment,* (9) *client retention services,* (10) *payroll and back-office administrative support,* and (11) *legislative compliance services.* Centralizing the administrative duties in a single mortgage transaction and over the mortgage life of a client should free up more time for brokers to spend with their clients. It will also allow them to originate and manage more clients. The same goes for accounting and compliance with regulations. It only makes good business sense to organize the responsibilities of an office and delegate the work accordingly.

Most small independent shops also have administrative support to look after these same responsibilities, and they are equally capable of performing their duties. Advancements in software technology have also played a key role in helping brokers and offices, large or small, run more efficiently.

(12) *Program/service innovation*. Superbrokerages have acquired the critical mass to forge affinity relationships with real estate and other organizations to drive in new business for their brokers. There may also be benefits to you, the consumer—for example, exclusive mortgage rates with "no frills" offered through the co-ordinated efforts of a bank, mortgage broker, and real estate company (e.g., the Sutton Mortgage Program). Also, most of the superbrokerages have either rolled out or are considering their own line of mortgages, also known as private-label mortgages.

Mortgage Intelligence was the first superbrokerage to offer private-label mortgages back in 2001, branded i-mortgages. They were funded through their parent company, GMAC, but were later shelved during the credit crunch. If you choose one of these, just be sure to read the fine print to learn what "no frills" means and understand what you are giving up. One of the trends in designing private-label mortgages is to strip down the features you, the consumer, don't need or perhaps don't think you need, to reach the lowest rate possible.

I may be from the old school, but I think this trend perpetuates the parochial business of selling rate. Be sure not to be railroaded into taking something without knowing what your options are. I also find it interesting to think consumers would have a strong desire for their mortgages to be labelled and sourced with a relatively unknown superbrokerage. Conventional wisdom would suggest otherwise. Right or wrong, the majority of Canadians still like to know their mortgages are safe and secure under the familiarity and strength of a few well-known financial institutions. After all, we're not selling suits.

(13) *Lender relationships*. The prevailing perception amongst both

the small independents and the superbrokerages is that national firms have more pull with the lenders. That is not to say lenders underwrite mortgages any differently, but when push comes to shove, do nationals have the executive muscle to make a difference? If I were a cynic, I might think so. After all, given the sheer size of their labour force, most lenders have had to organize their underwriting staff and allocate designated teams to service each superbrokerage.

From a strictly business standpoint, I have no problem with that kind of allocation of resources. Every lender endeavours to build consistency into their underwriting, and that includes the relationships between broker and underwriter. I have worked with far too many exemplary underwriters to suggest that I, a small independent, was left with second-best underwriting. Once again, to encourage volume business, some lenders will reward brokers who reach volume tiers, with a dedicated team to service all the broker's clients. As long as the underwriting guidelines are the same for everyone, I have no issues with this.

More recently, lenders have become obsessed with closing or efficiency ratios and other broker metrics. Brokers who don't care to understand a lender's requirements will and have been cut off. It has taken some time, but lenders are finally fed up with receiving applications that don't meet their criteria and are continually declining them.

Lenders have efficiency ratios set at 60%. For every ten deals submitted, six have to close, or fund. Anything less constitutes too much time and money spent on a file and a misuse of the lender's resources, which ends up costing everyone. It's about time. A closing ratio below the 60% cutoff demonstrates a lack of training at the brokerage house. And where do you think this occurs more often? The model with less supervision, of course, whose claims include having the best training. Go figure. Ask the underwriters and business development managers at most banks where most of the training for new brokers comes from. They are the ones left to do most of the training, and for free!

The vast majority of brokers who work for a superbrokerage are home-based and mobile. This is no different from the mobile mortgage representatives who work exclusively for one bank. If you prefer not to drive to an office just for a face-to-face meeting, your broker will come to you.

I have never worked for a superbrokerage, and my own brokerage company represents the small independent shop. I have a bias towards which organizational structure I prefer, but let me shed some light on some key differences you should know.

As mentioned, the vast majority of brokers/agents working for a superbrokerage works from home or out of the trunk of their cars. This mobile service may appeal to some, but it comes with some inherent dangers you should be aware of. The home-based superbroker is far less supervised than the average broker, a fact that attracts the attention of our government regulatory bodies. In Ontario, that is the Financial Services Commission of Ontario (FSCO). If you were to call the FSCO to ask about the number of complaints filed against mortgage brokers, guess who receives the majority of complaints?

I personally know some excellent mortgage brokers who work for a superbrokerage and there are many more like them. However, with the lack of built-in supervision, the superbrokerage model has attracted less scrupulous types. Does the drive to grow and become the biggest superbrokerage lead these organizations to relax their standards? My experience cited in the previous chapter is case in point. Yes, the broker I filed a complaint against worked for a superbrokerage.

This drive for market dominance at high commission splits for brokers, equity shares in the company, reduced margins, and lax ethical standards may be a model for accelerated growth and profitability, but I'm not so sure it's a model for success, at least not where the average broker and the consumer are concerned. Ask the many senior executives who have shuffled between superbrokerages in the last ten years or who left the broker side all together. Why did they move?

As for the small independent shops like mine, it's business as usual. Growth doesn't come at the expense of quality personnel and quality customer service. The two go hand in hand. We may not book as much business as the superbrokerages in a year, but just ask us where our next customer is likely to come from: existing client referrals and/or repeat clients. Now that's a model for success!

In the debate between superbrokerages and small independent shops, there may not be a clear winner yet. I happen to think both can coexist. This is a relationship business. As long as brokers serve clients well by putting client interests first, they will do okay, regardless of where they hang their hat. One thing is for sure: in the months and years ahead, we will continue to see changes to the mortgage broker channel.

CHAPTER 9

KNOW YOUR CREDIT

When you apply for a loan or mortgage, one of the first things a lender will do to see if you qualify is go to the credit bureau to determine your credit profile. Credit bureaus are private companies. Their business is the collection of financial data, provided by creditors, regarding the credit habits and history of consumers and businesses. Lenders often refer to the credit bureau's report as your credit rating.

With the exit of Experian Canada on April 17, 2009, only two credit bureaus remain in operation in Canada:

1. Equifax
2. TransUnion

Experts believe that over 95% of data from all the major creditors is reported to both Equifax and TransUnion. Traditionally, credit unions didn't report to either bureau, but that is changing. However, if you deal exclusively with a non-reporting credit grantor, you need to be aware that this means you won't have a credit rating, good or bad.

With their vast database and statistical rating system, the credit bureau can sum up your credit rating in one number, known as your credit score. Equifax calls it your Beacon score, TransUnion calls it your Empirica score. Both scoring models are virtually the same (both having been designed by the same company, Fair Isaac) and range from 300 to 900, 900 being perfect. In my career, the best I have ever seen was 850.

Credit scores, however, don't measure the creditworthiness of someone today. A credit score was designed to predict one or two years into the future. If you want a snapshot of today, you need to look at the whole credit report. For example, John is current and doesn't have any delinquencies on his credit report and yet only scores 580. He has ten fully utilized credit cards, he is seeking new credit, and the types of products that he is seeking are high risk. The whole concept of scoring is that past performance will predict future behaviour.

In addition to credit scores, some lenders have incorporated the credit bureau's score into their own statistical rating system to determine their own unique score. In addition, lenders may have custom application scorecards for different portfolios. For example, one scorecard may be used for lines of credit, another for loans, and yet another for mortgages.

It all sounds a bit confusing. What matters most is that many lenders now use auto-decision models built on minimum credit scores in their adjudication and rate setting process. It is therefore a great benefit to understand your credit profile and take the necessary steps to optimize your credit rating before applying for a mortgage. I recommend checking your own credit report at least four months in advance of applying for a mortgage. For a nominal fee, you can now check with both bureaus online to get your report instantaneously.

Below is a summary of methods for requesting your credit report and their respective characteristics:

Method	Advantages	Disadvantages
Mail	Free of charge	Credit score not provided
		Can take two or more weeks to receive
Internet	Report received immediately	Access requires a fee
	Option to also receive credit score	

DEVELOP A POSITIVE CREDIT PROFILE

The better you understand what statistics or categories are behind your score, the easier it will be for you to get credit. To develop a positive credit profile, qualify yourself in as many categories as you can in the list below (in order of importance):

1. A positive up-to-date credit report
2. A home with a mortgage
3. The age of your credit history
4. A job you have held for a year or more
5. A current or paid-off bank loan
6. A major credit card
7. A department store credit card
8. A telephone in your name

Other factors influencing your credit profile (which you may or may not have control over):

• The amount of debt you have relative to your income
• Your net worth
• Your age
• You have a chequing and/or savings account (chequing and saving accounts are not reported to the credit bureau, but derogatory

banking information may be)

- Length of time at current and previous residence
- The number of credit cards you hold
- The number of times you applied for credit in the past six months

Always remember, a positive up-to-date credit file, listed above as the number one influence on your credit profile, is *your responsibility*, not the credit bureaus'. Furthermore, it's something you create, not something that happens automatically.

CREDIT BUREAU FILE CONTROL STRATEGIES

- *Check your credit bureau file once a year.* Your credit report is prepared for you in simple language without all the jargon and rating codes only a lender or mortgage broker would understand. If you need help interpreting your report, ask your mortgage broker.

- *Have the credit bureau re-verify and correct any inaccurate personal and credit data.* The credit bureau has an obligation to use its best efforts to check and correct the file. You can request that a correction be made to your file either by phone, in person, or online. Providing official supporting documentation can correct personal information. The credit bureau can correct credit information after it conducts an investigation with the credit grantor who reported the information.

- *Have all missing positive credit data added to your file.* Supply the credit bureau with a list in writing of all credit cards, loans, and mortgages you have kept current if they are missing from your credit file.

- *Add your story to the file.* You have the legal right to add your side of the story to your credit file, including reasons why your payments were late or that credit data is incorrect and is being re-verified.

- *Have the credit bureau remove any derogatory information outside the statutory limits.* You have the legal right to a credit file that doesn't contain data older than the statutory limits.

One of the most common questions asked about credit reports is, "How long do the credit bureaus keep information in my credit file?" The answer varies depending on the nature of the information. For example, credit inquiries may be purged after three to five years, while credit history and banking information may be removed after six years. Collection accounts under public record may be purged after six years. Bankruptcies may be purged after six years from the date of discharge, though multiple bankruptcies may require up to fourteen years each. Contact one of the credit bureaus for clarification and further details regarding the purging of the information that appears in your report.

WARNINGS, MYTHS, AND MISCONCEPTIONS

First, make no mistake about who has access to your credit file. Federal and provincial laws are very specific as to who can review your credit file and for what purpose. An individual or company may only obtain a copy of your credit file with your consent or after having told you that they will be reviewing your file. A company must have a legitimate business reason and a permissible purpose, as stated in government regulations, to obtain your credit file.

When you apply for a loan or credit card, you are usually asked to complete and sign an application form. An application normally includes written consent that gives permission to the credit grantor to check your credit file when you first apply and for as long as the account is open. In addition to your name, an application often asks for your date of birth, your address, and a previous address if you've recently moved, all of which help locate your credit file at a credit reporting agency.

Each time a member of the credit bureau requests your file, the request is noted on your file as an inquiry. You can therefore see a complete record of who has requested your credit file and when.

A credit reporting agency may only provide a copy of your file when the request relates to the extension of credit, a collection of a debt, a housing rental, an application for employment, or for insurance purposes. Since your credit file contains only factual information, it's important to remember that each of the companies requesting your credit file will interpret those facts in its own way to arrive at a decision. Of course, you also have the right to obtain a copy of your credit report.

I should mention that, with the exception of a secured line of credit, mortgages are not currently reported to the credit bureaus. This may change. The credit bureaus completed all of the necessary IT testing and preparation to receive and disseminate the mortgage data years ago. It would appear to me that the banks are the ones reluctant to participate in reporting the data. Mortgages are the coveted credit prize of every lender. If this information becomes available on your credit report, efforts to solicit your mortgage business away from your current lender will increase.

REBUILDING YOUR CREDIT

Whether it's after a bankruptcy or a run of misfortune, rebuilding your credit is essentially the same. Lenders tend to want to see about two years of re-established credit with sound money-management patterns, good savings, and credit repayment. If you went bankrupt, you also need to be two years past your discharged date if you are interested in traditional mortgage lending. Keep this in mind if you are considering a consumer proposal instead of bankruptcy. Briefly, a proposal is a legal procedure where a consumer offers to repay a portion of the outstanding debt. That portion might be as low as ten cents on the dollar or as much as the entire debt. A consumer proposal is for a maximum of five years. Just as with a bankruptcy, you are discharged from the consumer proposal at the end of the term.

The problem with consumer proposals is that banks will treat you the same as someone who claimed bankruptcy—you need to be discharged. If you went bankrupt, you could potentially re-enter the mortgage market two years after your discharge date, depending on how well you re-established your credit. If you went with a consumer proposal, you may not be able to re-enter the mortgage market for up to seven years—five years during the consumer proposal and another two years after your discharge. So much for doing the responsible thing and trying to make restitution.

But what about non-traditional mortgage lending? Yes, for a price, there is always a lender willing to take on the added risk. Some lenders will give you a mortgage one day out of bankruptcy and one day after a proposal has been satisfied. Along with lender fees and higher rates, you will also need a minimum down payment of 25%. Even more rare are the lenders who will give you a mortgage while you are still in a consumer proposal and allow the consumer proposal to continue. Most lenders will want you to pay the remaining debt as a condition of the mortgage. If the debt is too large, there won't be enough money to do anything else. The most rare of all is the lender who will let you continue in your consumer proposal and give you a mortgage. Your proposal repayment history will need to be perfect and at least two years old.

The limits you acquire on your new credit are also important. You may have to start small by virtue of what you have to secure it with or what the lender is willing to grant you. Your credit limit on any one trade (e.g., a credit card) will have to reach at least $1,500 before it will have any real impact on your credit score. Be patient!

CHAPTER 10

Insurance

People toss around the term *mortgage insurance* and can cause some confusion. There are four completely different types of insurance you need to know about when getting a mortgage: life, disability, title, and default. The first two have to do with your health, while the other two have to do with your property.

LIFE AND DISABILITY INSURANCE

Any time you get a loan, whether it's a big one secured by a mortgage or an unsecured personal loan, every lender will want you to take out some life and/or disability insurance, the premiums for which will be added to your monthly loan payment. In the case of life insurance against your mortgage, in the event of your premature death, the insurance will pay off the outstanding balance on your mortgage. This is referred to as declining balance coverage.

If you want a bigger bang for your buck, you can also get regular term insurance, which will pay out a certain amount regardless of what is left on your mortgage. For example, if you die with $100,000 left on your mortgage but your policy was for $200,000 (the amount your original mortgage likely started at), the insurance company pays your beneficiary $200,000. Your beneficiary will decide what to do with the money. They can pay off the mortgage and pocket the remaining $100,000 or they can keep the mortgage going and pocket the $200,000. In my experience, banks only offer the declining balance. What's worse, the insurance policy is in the bank's name and you must pay off the mortgage upon death, whether you want to or not.

The other disadvantage of getting your mortgage life insurance through the bank is that the insurance policy will expire if you leave that bank. This limits your options at renewal time or if you want to refinance with another lender. For example, most of the main banks have "switch programs" that enable you to change to another more competitive bank at renewal time at no cost. However, if you obtained your mortgage life insurance policy through Bank A, it will expire when you move to Bank B. You can apply again, but if your health has changed for the worse, you could be facing a higher monthly premium or, even worse, the bank could deny coverage all together. Your age has also increased in the meantime and that may put you in a higher risk/premium category.

Avoid all of this by setting up your life and disability insurance coverage separate from the bank holding your mortgage. Having coverage with an independent insurance company puts the policy in your name, not the bank's, so you can switch lenders at renewal time or during a refinance without affecting your policy whatsoever. Moreover, with the policy in your name, you can decide how the money is spent.

In my experience, the banks always seem to be more expensive anyway. They lure people into thinking it's more convenient to have it included with their mortgage payment. I don't know about you, but there is no difference to me whether the bank or an insurance company debits my account for the insurance premium. That's the beauty of pre-authorized debits.

What I hate the most is when clients tell me the lender put the insurance on automatically and the client thought they had to take the insurance. Life and disability insurance on your mortgage is always optional; it's never a condition of getting the loan, unless you are dealing with a private lender, because they have a little more freedom to impose whatever conditions they are comfortable with. For example, if you are self-employed, they may want you to have coverage.

In the case of disability insurance on your mortgage, if you have an accident and are off work, the insurance company will continue to make your mortgage payments for up to two years. You may or may not have insurance coverage of this kind through your employer. If you do, they usually only cover up to 60% of your income, which may not be enough to cover all your bills, including your mortgage payment.

A qualified insurance broker is the best person to speak with when considering your options for health insurance coverage with your mortgage. If you don't know one, ask your mortgage broker.

TITLE INSURANCE

It's difficult to get a mortgage today without the lender requiring a title insurance policy to be taken out and paid for by the borrower. It's not a provincial requirement to have title insurance, but lenders are free to establish their own policies. There is no extra legwork involved, as your lawyer will take care of it and include the cost in with the legal bill.

The word *title* is a legal term that refers to the legal ownership of a property. When a property owner signs the deed (transfer document) over to you, the title becomes yours and is registered in the government's land registration system. Title insurance, therefore, is an insurance policy that protects property owners and their lenders against losses related to the property's title or ownership.

For a one-time fee (usually around $300), a title insurance policy may provide protection against such losses as:

- unknown title defects (title issues that prevent you from having clear ownership of the property);

- existing liens against the property's title (e.g., the previous owner had unpaid debts from utilities, mortgages, property taxes, or condominium charges secured against the property);

- encroachment issues (e.g., a structure on your property needs to be removed because it's on your neighbour's property);

- title fraud;

- errors in surveys and public records; and

- other title-related issues that can affect your ability to sell, mortgage, or lease your property in the future.

Your title insurance policy will protect you as long as you own your property and will cover losses up to the maximum coverage set out in the policy. It may also cover most legal expenses related to restoring your property's title.

Title fraud has become increasingly common in today's real estate market. It typically involves a fraudster using stolen personal information or forged documents to transfer your property's title to him or herself (or an accomplice) without your knowledge. The fraudster then takes out a mortgage on your home and disappears with the money.

If you are a victim of title fraud, you may be able to receive compensation for your losses if you submit a claim through the government's Land Titles Assurance Fund (LTAF). For more information on the Land Titles Assurance Fund, visit the Ontario government's website (www.ontario.ca) and search for "Land Titles Assurance Fund," as the URL is too long to repeat here.

There are two main types of title insurance policies:

1. *Owner's policy.* This protects the property owner from the various title-related losses listed in the insurance policy for as long as the property is owned. An owner's policy sets a maximum amount of coverage.

2. *Lender's policy.* This protects the lender from losses in the event that the property's mortgage is invalid or unenforceable. A lender's policy usually provides coverage for the amount of the property's mortgage.

Lenders who require you to have title insurance as a condition of the loan might only instruct your lawyer to obtain a lender's policy. Don't assume you are also getting an owner's policy—you might have to advise your lawyer accordingly. If you're not sure, ask your mortgage broker.

What about refinancing with the same lender who had you take out a lender's policy on your mortgage the first time? Do you need to pay for another policy? Yes, but the cost for a policy on a refinance is less.

DEFAULT INSURANCE

The final type of insurance you may or may not need is mortgage default insurance. This depends on how much equity you have in your home if you are an existing homeowner doing a refinance. If you are a homebuyer, it depends on how much money you are putting down on the purchase price. In Canada, all lenders regulated under the *Bank Act* must comply with regulations and obtain default insurance any time a mortgage exceeds 80% of a property's value.

Mortgage default insurance protects *the lender* in the event you default on your mortgage and force the lender to sell the property. If the sale proceeds are insufficient to cover the lender's selling costs and outstanding mortgage balance, the insurance will cover the loss.

You can default on your mortgage in many ways; however, this insurance is primarily concerned with your defaulting by not making your mortgage payments, which can lead to a power of sale or foreclosure.

Canadian mortgage delinquencies don't typically turn into foreclosures until they are at least three months in arrears and the lender has exhausted all other default-management avenues. If foreclosure is unavoidable, a judicial sale of the property (in which a court supervises the home sale) occurs in British Columbia, Alberta, Saskatchewan, Manitoba, and Quebec. A power of sale (in which the lender sells the property without supervision) occurs in Ontario, New Brunswick, Prince Edward Island, and Newfoundland. Nova Scotia uses a mix of the two approaches. If the sale proceeds from the house are in excess of the mortgage and administrative fees, the lender pockets the excess amount in the case of a judicial sale, while the borrower keeps the excess funds in the case of a power of sale.

Mortgages that exceed the 80% financing threshold are deemed at a higher risk of going into this kind of default and must be protected by the insurance. Before 2009, if you purchased a home in Canada, federal law required you have a 25% down payment. Financing beyond 75% was considered too risky. With the price of homes continually moving up over time, raising the 25% mandatory down payment became more difficult for most people to do. In response, the government developed the default insurance program, which allowed Canadians to borrow beyond 75% of the property's purchase price. Lenders could now take the added risk and offer high-ratio loans (greater than 75% LTV) with the protection of default insurance.

I hope I haven't confused you with these LTV limits. At the beginning, I said all lenders regulated under the *Bank Act* must comply with the regulations and obtain default insurance any time the mortgage exceeds 80% of the property's value. I also referred to a 75% threshold. When the 1954 *National Housing Act* first introduced default insurance, the threshold was 66.67%. In 1965, they increased the statutory limit to 75%. Most recently, on April 20, 2007, an amendment to the *Bank Act* increased the limit to 80%.

Although default insurance protection is for the lender, *the borrower* pays the cost of the insurance. In the case of a purchase, the one-time fee or insurance premium is based on the size of your down payment. The less you put down, the greater the cost of the insurance. The insurance premiums (and associated administration fees) have changed over the years along with the maximum allowed financing. The table of premiums below gives the current pricing:

Premium on Total Loan   Premium on Increase to Loan Amount for Portability and Refinance

	Standard Premium	Self-Employed without Third-Party Income Validation *	Standard Premium	Self-Employed without Third-Party Income Validation **
Up to and including 65%	0.50%	0.80%	0.50%	1.50%
Up to and including 75%	0.65%	1.00%	2.25%	2.60%
Up to and including 80%	1.00%	1.64%	2.75%	3.85%
Up to and including 85%	1.75%	2.90%	3.50%	5.50%
Up to and including 90%	2.00%	4.75%	4.25%*	7.00%*
Up to and including 95%	2.75%	N/A	4.25%*	*
90.01% to 95% –				
Non-Traditional Down Payment***	2.90%	N/A	*	N/A

Extended Amortization Surcharges

Add 0.20% for every five years of amortization beyond the 25-year mortgage amortization period.†

For portability and refinance, the premium is the lesser of Premium on Increase to Loan Amount or the Premium on Total Loan Amount. In the case of portability, a premium credit may be available under certain conditions.

* Premiums shown with an "**" do not apply for refinance. For portability, the premium is higher for non-traditional down payments on Increase to Loan Amount.

** Premiums shown with an "**" do not apply for refinance. For portability, the maximum LTV ratio is 90%, but CMHC may consider higher LTV ratios when the new ratio is equal to or less than the original LTV. For portability, the premium is higher for non-traditional third-party income validation on Increase to Loan Amount.

** For conversion from Self-Employed with traditional third-party income validation to Self-Employed without traditional third-party income validation, the premium is the lesser of: a) the Premium on Total Loan Amount, or b) the outstanding balance multiplied by a 1.5% premium plus the Premium on Increase to Loan Amount.

*** Down Payment Requirements – Traditional sources of down payment include: Applicant's savings, RRSP withdrawal, funds borrowed against proven assets, sweat equity (<50% of minimum required equity), land unencumbered, proceeds from sale of another property, non-repayable gift from immediate relative, equity grant (non-re-payable grant from federal, provincial, or municipal agency). Non-traditional sources of down payment include: Any source that is arm's length to and not tied to the purchase or sale of the property, such as borrowed funds, gifts, 100% sweat equity, lender cash back incentives.

† The amortization cannot exceed thirty years for mortgage LTV ratios > 80%.

Premiums in Ontario and Quebec are subject to provincial sales tax. The provincial sales tax cannot be added to the loan amount.

Source: Canada Mortgage and Housing Corporation

Before the 2008 subprime mortgage fiasco and subsequent credit crunch, the maximum allowed financing was 100%. That's right. You could buy a house with zero down payment. Although largely a problem associated with the U.S., the 2008 credit crunch changed the way mortgages were underwritten both in the U.S. and Canada to prevent any chance of a reoccurrence and to restore the health and liquidity of the banking community. For example, the maximum allowable financing on a purchase returned to 95% on October 15, 2008. Many more changes followed, such as:

- The maximum amortization reduced to thirty-five years, and then again shortly after to thirty years.

- The maximum allowable financing on a refinance dropped to 90%, and then again shortly after to 85%.

- Homebuyers now have to qualify at the 5-year posted rate for terms less than five years.

Competition in the mortgage default insurance market is slim. In economics, they refer to this as an oligopoly, which is a market structure in which a market or industry is dominated by a small number of sellers who recognize their mutual interdependence. With few insurance providers, the decisions of one firm influence and are influenced by the decisions of other firms. The only thing worse than an oligopoly is a monopoly. If you haven't studied economics, all you need to know is what these market forms represent. The bottom line is that we are all paying too much for the service provided by these firms due to the lack of competition in the industry.

There are currently only three providers of mortgage default insurance in Canada:

1. Canada Mortgage and Housing Corporation (CMHC)

2. Genworth Financial Canada
3. AIG United Guaranty

These companies represent a classic oligopoly if ever there was one. However, the situation gets even worse than simple market structure. Exactly how they charge you for mortgage default insurance is less than fair, in my opinion. Mortgage default insurance is expensive. For a purchase, the borrower pays a one-time premium *on the total amount of the mortgage* and not just on the portion exceeding 80% of the purchase price—the high-ratio portion that increased the risk of default. Remember, you don't need the insurance for mortgages up to 80% LTV. Depending on the size of your down payment, the insurance premiums range from 1.75% to 2.90% between 80% and 95%.

For example, if you purchase a house for $300,000 and you can put down 20%, you don't need mortgage default insurance, and your mortgage would look like this:

Purchase price	$300,000
Less: down payment (@ 20%)	60,000
Equals total mortgage (@ 80%)	$240,000

What if you can only put down $55,000? You will only mortgage $5,000 more ($245,000), and the risk of default only goes up by $5,000. The fair cost of insurance should reflect the added $5,000 risk. Instead, they apply the cost of the insurance against the total loan amount ($245,000). Your mortgage would look like this:

Purchase price	$300,000
Less: down payment (@18.33%)	55,000
Equals net mortgage (@ 81.67%)	$245,000
Plus: insurance premium ($245,000 X 1.75%)	$4,288
Equals total mortgage	$249,288

Most people need every last penny they've saved to come up with their down payment and closing costs and will elect to have the mortgage default insurance premium added to their mortgage as shown in the table above. This option is available and is used 99.99% of the time. However, this means paying additional interest on the cost of the insurance and with the added cost of having your equity position depleted by the same amount of the premium.

A better, more equitable practice would be to base the cost of the insurance on the added risk (that portion of the mortgage above the 80% threshold). You would pay it on a monthly basis like life and disability. Best of all, you could cancel it at any time if you could prove your mortgage was no longer greater than 80% of the property's value. That would be easy to prove. Property values rise most often. In addition, your outstanding mortgage balance will drop with each regular scheduled mortgage payment you make. Before long, you could pay for an appraisal to determine the market value of your house. As soon as your mortgage drops to 80% or less of the appraised value, you could cancel the insurance.

Why aren't we doing this? This isn't merely the musing of an old cranky mortgage broker. This has been widely practiced in the U.S. for some time. It's about time Canadians stood up for themselves and fought for a better deal. The problem is that there aren't many consumer advocate groups around taking up the cause. I might also suggest that our oligopolistic friends listed above are making very good money under the current system.

But don't feel bad. Until now, I haven't done anything about it either, and I have known about it for some time. I am therefore starting an online petition. If you sign my petition, I pledge to take our names as far as I can go to effect the necessary change. We need a fair system as I described above, and we need more providers (insurers) to make sure the service is price competitive.

Please go to www.MortgageResource.ca/petition to sign the petition.

If you are not yet convinced that we need a better system, allow me to point out a few more problems inherent in the current system. Take, for example, homebuyers who purchased a new home one or two years in advance of its construction—a "new build," as we like to call them. When the agreement of purchase and sale was written up and signed, the purchase price was $285,000. My clients could only come up with a 15% down payment. Less than 20% means they had to pay for default insurance. At 85% financing, the cost of the insurance was $4,239.38: the insurance premium (1.75%) multiplied by the whole loan amount ($242,250).

When the homebuyers were ready to move into their newly built home one or two years later, the builder was asking $350,000 for the exact same model home they purchased, a value supported by the appraisal the homebuyers were required to get just before closing when the home was at least 97% complete. The homebuyers' mortgage ($242,250) now represented only 69.21% of the property's current appraised value. So when their mortgage finally closed on moving day, they essentially had a conventional mortgage (less than 80% of the property's current value) that didn't require default insurance—but they had to pay for it anyway. Why?

Confounding the problem is bank policy, which is to always lend against the lesser amount between the purchase price and the appraisal. The purchase price one or two years earlier is going to be less in a real estate market with typical growth, so the homebuyers had to pay default insurance on what turned out to be a conventional loan. A mortgage default insurance system that supports current appraised values would avoid this problem.

In this situation, I advised my clients to borrow the extra 5% needed to avoid the default insurance ($14,250). We arranged a fully open mortgage to close, and one day later refinanced the mortgage (with no penalty and no extra legal costs) and rolled in the extra 5% they had to borrow. The new bigger mortgage ($242,250 + $14,250 = $256,500) was still conventional (less than 80%) based on the current appraised value ($350,000) and consequently didn't require the default insurance.

Okay, now please go to www.MortgageResource.ca/petition to sign the petition.

And while I'm at it, there is one more thing that really gets me. If you pay for default insurance (and pay handsomely), in the event of a default and subsequent power of sale or foreclosure, if the insurer has to pay to cover a loss (i.e., the sale proceeds don't cover the mortgage amount outstanding), they will register a judgement against you, the homeowner, to recover their money. So what do you pay the insurance for? Yes, I know the protection is for the lender, and they receive the payout from the insurer to cover their loss, but *you* pay for this insurance protection. Can you think of any other case where you pay for insurance protection, have the insurance company cover a loss, only to have them file a judgement against you to recover the money?

That's quite the business they're running.

Okay, last time: please go to www.MortgageResource.ca/petition to sign the petition.

CHAPTER 11

NUMBER CRUNCHING

There is a reason why this chapter appears near the end of the book. If I started the book with this chapter, my guess is that most readers wouldn't likely see the rest of it. Most of us don't like to do math, but the hard truth is that it's a requirement. Buying homes is very much about the emotional experience and lifestyle decisions you make. But when the dust settles and you are left to pay the bills, the love affair you have with your new home may start to fade.

The good news is you don't have to be good with numbers. Just sit down with someone who is and make sure they do a good job going over the affordability of your new home. Your mortgage broker is your best source for addressing the costs associated with buying and owning your home.

DEBT SERVICE RATIOS

To qualify for a mortgage, banks look at the five Cs: credit, character, capacity, collateral, and, believe it or not, common sense. Some banks do a better job than others with the final C. All five factors have their place in the underwriting decision of your loan application, but capacity, or your ability to repay, will address affordability.

Along with job stability and employability, capacity is also a measure of your ability to repay the loan based on your income. The general rule for how much mortgage you can afford has always been around 2.5% of your gross household income. If you and your spouse together bring in a gross income of $100,000, you would qualify for a mortgage of around $250,000. This number can be pared back if you are carrying a significant amount of other debts (e.g., car loans, credit cards, etc.) Assuming your other debts are minimal, if you have $30,000 to use as your down payment, that puts you on target for a house priced at $280,000 ($250,000 + $30,000). Pretty straight-forward, no?

Of course, general rules become outdated over time. This one was largely based on using the typical 25-year amortization and when the average interest rate for a 5-year term was over 11%. Today, however, banks allow up to 40-year amortizations on conventional loans and we are seeing much lower rates. It would therefore be a good idea to sit down with your mortgage broker to see exactly how much you can afford based on today's rules and your own personal set of circumstances.

General rules are good for breaking the ice, but when it comes time to underwrite your loan application, the rules are stricter. In addition to the aforementioned terms, your capacity to repay the loan must meet strict debt service ratios, meaning your debt-to-income ratios cannot exceed a capped percentage. For most banks, your shelter costs cannot exceed 32% of your gross household income. This includes the cost of your mortgage payment, which consists of principal and interest (P and I); property taxes (T); and heating (H)— also referred to as PITH—plus 50% of your monthly condo fees (if applicable). They refer to this as your gross debt service ratio (GDSR). They also look at your total debt service ratio (TDSR), which looks at your shelter costs plus any other debts you have (e.g., car loan, credit cards, etc.), and it cannot exceed 42% of your gross household income.

A good place to start your quest to buy a home is with your capacity to repay. If your GDSR and TDSR fall below the limits, you know you can afford the house. All you have to do now is clear the remaining hurdles (the remaining four Cs) and have the minimum required down payment to get approved.

In the following example, Mr. and Mrs. Smith are interested in buying a freehold property for $400,000. The following table summarizes their financial profile and the carrying costs associated with the house:

Gross monthly household income (before tax)	$10,833
Other monthly debts (e.g., car loans, credit cards, etc.)	$1,500
Monthly property taxes on house	$333
Monthly heating cost on house (estimate)	$150
Down payment	$80,000

You will notice that their down payment is 20% of the $400,000 purchase price. For the purpose of this example, I have conveniently left out the cost of default insurance. Therefore, the Smiths' conventional mortgage (uninsured) will be $320,000 ($400,000 - $80,000). Using a 25-year amortization and a 5-year fixed rate of 4.35%, their monthly mortgage payment is $1,745. Now we can calculate their debt service ratios as follows:

GDSR = (PITH + 50% condo fees / gross household income) x 100

Remembering to keep everything in monthly terms, this translates to:

GDSR = ($1,745 + $333 + $150 / $10,833) x 100 = 20.57%

The GDSR is well below the 32% limit,—so far so good for Mr. and Mrs. Smith. Next is the TDSR:

$$TDSR = (PITH + 50\% \text{ condo fees} + \text{all other debts} /$$
$$\text{gross household income}) \times 100$$

$$= (\$1,745 + \$333 + \$150 + \$1,500 / \$10,833) \times 100$$

$$= 34.41\%$$

The TDSR is well below the 42% limit. With both debt service ratios in line, Mr. and Mrs. Smith have proven they can easily afford the $400,000 freehold home. Now all they have to do is qualify under the other four Cs and they will be approved for the $320,000 mortgage.

CLOSING COSTS

The closing costs associated with buying a house are something that first-time homebuyers often forget about. So much attention is focused on raising the down payment that they forget about closing costs. If you are a qualified first-time homebuyer, there are some financial breaks to reduce your closing costs that I will discuss later, but first, I wish to cover the entire list of closing costs everyone else needs to be aware of. Along with the list of costs in the table below, I have also provided, where applicable, an estimate of the dollar value based on my experience in and around the Greater Toronto Area. Some of the costs (e.g., default insurance, PST, etc.) will be bang on.

Note that default insurance providers in Canada, such as Canada Mortgage and Housing Corporation (CMHC), are deemed insurance agents and are exempt from HST under the *Excise Tax Act*, a part of what Revenue Canada calls a selected list of financial institutions (SLFI). For participating provinces, the HST replaces all provincial retail sales taxes (RST or PST) and the GST. Since the HST follows the same rules as the outgoing federal GST with regard to SLFI exemptions, there is no HST on default insurance in any province. However, some provinces, not wanting to give up the revenue, have continued their application of a retail sales tax, or PST. The only provinces doing this are Ontario and Quebec. The rest of the country pays no tax on default insurance. Way to go, Ontario and Quebec.

The below example will show an Ontario purchase transaction with a high ratio, where an insured mortgage (default insurance) is required. The first-time homebuyers in this example will be putting down 5% of the purchase price for a house in Toronto. The following table is one I provide to all my clients. It gives them a heads up on the closing costs they will likely encounter at their lawyer's office on closing day.

The Costs Associated with Buying a Home

Purchase price	$400,000
Plus	
Home inspection fee	$400
Appraisal fee	$200
Default mortgage insurance premium	$10,450
PST on default mortgage insurance premium (8% in Ontario)	$836
Property survey or title insurance fee	$350
Legal fees (for purchase, mortgage, and disbursements)	$1,200
Mortgage broker fee (if applicable)	$0
Lender's fee (if applicable)	$0
Ontario land transfer tax (LTT)	$4,475
Less LTT refund for first-time homebuyers (max. $2,000)	($2,000)
Toronto land transfer tax	$3,725
Property tax holdback (varies with lender; can be up to six months)	$2,000
Other adjustments (interest, utilities, condo fees, etc.)	$300
Equals	
Total estimated purchase cost	$421,936

How much money do you need to cover closing costs?

Total estimated purchase cost	$421,936
Less	
Down payment: (choose applicable sources)	
Savings (including deposit with offer to purchase)	$20,000
Equity from sale of previous house (or bridge loan)	
RRSP and/or other investments	
Gift (from family or cash back incentive from lender)	
Financing arranged with lender	$390,450
Equals	
Total estimated closing cost*	$11,486

- Your lawyer will call you before your scheduled visit to confirm the amount of money you need to have available. Give yourself enough time to have this amount put in your bank account, as your lawyer will only accept a certified cheque. The only exception is equity coming from the sale of your existing home if you are closing the same day on both properties.

For new construction only:

Check with your lawyer regarding any closing costs specific to the builder (e.g., home warranty costs, development charges, etc.)

There are other closing costs to deal with outside of your lawyer's office. They include:

- House fire insurance premium
- Moving expenses
- Appliances
- Utilities and cable installation charges
- Immediate repairs

For greater clarification, let me point out a few things from our purchase example above. First, notice that the total estimated purchase cost is $421,936. That's $21,936 above the purchase price needed to buy the house. Before you hit the panic button, understand the difference between purchase costs and closing costs. To determine the closing costs, we subtract the down payment and the mortgage provided by the lender, which in this case includes the default insurance. What's left over is the money our first-time homebuyers are responsible for to close the deal ($11,486). In fact, we could reduce it a bit more, since the first two costs (home inspection and appraisal) are paid for up front, long before closing day. Furthermore, in the case of an insured mortgage, like in this example, there is no appraisal cost. The default insurance company (e.g., CMHC) doesn't require it. The home inspection is optional, although I would not recommend opting out of it.

Subtracting the home inspection and appraisal costs brings the total estimated closing costs to $10,886, or 2.72% of the purchase price. Another good rule of thumb is to budget between 2% and 3% for closing costs. A few things such as property tax holdbacks or additional builder costs in the case of a new build can easily fluctuate the percentage. The $10,886 is a good estimate of the closing costs for these first-time homebuyers as they prepare to close the deal.

The first-time homebuyers likely put down a deposit with the offer to purchase. In this price range and sellers' market, it would perhaps be as much as $10,000. This means on closing day, they will need to bring with them the balance of their down payment ($10,000) plus our estimate of closing costs ($10,886). That's a total of $20,886.

FIRST-TIME HOMEBUYER INCENTIVES

If you qualify as a first-time homebuyer, there are a few financial incentives to help you get into the housing market. Outlined below are both federal and provincial incentives offered for qualified first-time homebuyers. There are many more financial incentives available provincially that are not exclusive to first-time homebuyers. They are for existing homeowners looking to upgrade their homes to be more energy efficient, programs geared towards low-income Canadians, seniors, and homeowners with disabilities. You should visit your provincial government's website for more information. An extensive list of all the programs are also listed at www.MortgageResource.ca.

All of Canada

First-Time Home Buyers' Tax Credit (HBTC)
The HBTC is a non-refundable tax credit for certain homebuyers who acquire a qualifying home after January 27, 2009 (closing after this date). It was designed to assist first-time homebuyers with closing costs. The credit will provide up to $750 in federal tax relief.

For more information, call 1-800-959-8281 or visit www.cra-arc.gc.ca/nwsrm/fctshts/2010/m01/fs100121-eng.html.

GST/HST New Housing Rebate
Through the Canada Revenue Agency, the Canadian government administers the GST/HST New Housing Rebate program, which provides a rebate on the amount paid toward GST on a new construction home. Newly built homes and those that have undergone substantial renovations are eligible for the rebate. Substantial renovations include building an addition on the home and the rebuilding required if a fire severely damaged a home. Rebate amounts equal up to 1.5% of the GST paid on a home with a value of less than $350,000. Homes valued between $350,000 and $450,000 are eligible for a reduced rebate, while homes valued higher than $450,000 do not qualify for any rebate.

For more information contact Canada Revenue Agency at 1-800-959-2221 or visit www.cra-arc.gc.ca.

RRSP Home Buyers' Plan (HBP)

The Home Buyers' Plan (HBP) is a program that allows you to withdraw up to $25,000 (after January 27, 2009) from your Registered Retirement Savings Plan (RRSP) to buy or build a qualifying home for yourself or for a related person with a disability. The program is restricted to first-time homebuyers only.

For more information, visit www.cra-arc.gc.ca/tx/ndvdls/tpcs/rrsp-reer/hbp-rap/menu-eng.html.

British Columbia

Property Transfer Tax and the First-Time Home Buyers' Program

Introduced in 1994, the First-Time Home Buyers' Program is designed to help British Columbians purchase their first home. Under the program, eligible purchasers can claim an exemption from property transfer tax if the fair market value of the home is less than the threshold amount. For registrations on or after February 20, 2008, the fair market value threshold for eligible residential property is $425,000. A proportional exemption is provided for eligible residences with a fair market value of up to $25,000 above the threshold (i.e., up to $450,000).

For more information, contact the Ministry of Finance at 1-800-663-7867 (or locally at 250-387-0604) or e-mail PTTENQ @gov.bc.ca.

Manitoba

Land Transfer Tax Exemption for First-Time Homebuyers

Under the Land Titles system in effect in Manitoba, the province keeps a registry of land titles. Transferees are required to pay a land transfer tax and a registration fee at the nearest land titles office upon registration of transfer of title. First-time purchasers of residential property are exempt from paying the land transfer tax.

For more information, contact the Winnipeg Land Title Office at 204-945-2042.

Ontario

Land Transfer Tax Refunds for First-Time Homebuyers

In addition to being a first-time homebuyer, there are some restrictions to qualify for a land transfer tax refund. This program is available for newly constructed homes and resale homes purchased after December 13, 2007. The maximum refund is $2,000.

For additional information, please contact the Ontario Ministry of Revenue's Land and Resource Taxes section at 1-866-ONT-TAXS (1-866-668-8297) or visit www.rev.gov.on.ca/en/bulletins/ltt/1_2008.html.

Canada-Ontario Affordable Housing Program (AHP)

On April 29, 2005, the federal and provincial governments signed a new Canada-Ontario Affordable Housing Program (AHP). This program was developed to assist low-to-moderate-income rental households in purchasing affordable homes. Under the homeownership component of the AHP, down payment assistance will be 5% of the cost of an eligible home.

For more information, contact Canada-Ontario Affordable Housing Program, Delivery Branch at 416-585-6437 or visit www.mah.gov.on.ca/AssetFactory.aspx?did=4083.

New Brunswick

Home Ownership Program

This program is offered by the Department of Social Development (SD). It provides financial assistance to low- and modest-income families to help them buy or build a modest first home. This is available to families or individuals with total household incomes below $40,000 and who can obtain private financing such that when combined with the funding would result in the total acquisition/construction of the unit.

For more information, contact the regional housing office in your area.

Nova Scotia

First-Time Home Buyers HST Rebate

This rebate is available to buyers of newly constructed homes and is equivalent to 18.75% of the provincial portion of the HST (or 1.5% of the purchase price), to a maximum of $1,500 per home.

For more information, contact the Nova Scotia Tax Commission directly at 1-800-556-2336 or locally at (902) 424-2850.

Family Modest Housing Program

This program is designed to provide funds for lower- and middle-income families to build or buy modest housing. A mortgage of up to $70,000 is available.

For more information, contact the nearest Housing Services office of the Department of Community Services.

Prince Edward Island

Real Property Transfer Tax – First-Time Home Buyers Exemption

The Real Property Transfer Tax Act requires that every person registering a deed in Prince Edward Island pay a tax equal to 1% of the greater of the purchase price or the assessed value of the real property. Certain types of real property transfers are exempt from this tax. For instance, no tax is payable on the registration of a deed of conveyance if the purchaser is a first-time homebuyer.

For more information, contact Taxation and Property Records Division of the Department of Finance and Municipal Affairs at 902-368-4171 or taxandland@gov.pe.ca, or visit www.taxandland.pe.ca.

Quebec

Home Ownership Program

This program provides financial assistance to first-time buyers for the purchase of certain types of residential units in Montreal. Buyers must occupy the property as their principal residence. This program is funded jointly by the Quebec government and the City of Montreal under the Rénovation Québec program. For other municipalities, please check with your local city hall to see if they offer similar rebate programs.

For more information, visit www.habitermontreal.qc.ca.

CHAPTER 12

PRIVATE MORTGAGES

I have already covered the differences between prime and subprime mortgages and the many institutional lenders set up to handle both types. Using the risk continuum analogy from before, private mortgages (the most risky) would occupy one end of the continuum while prime mortgages (the least risky) would occupy the other end.

Institutional prime mortgage lenders use the most complete, formal, and conservative borrower qualification practices. They serve a reinvestment function (lending or investing funds "borrowed" from depositors or policy holders) and restrict their lending activities to first mortgage loans either well secured (80% LTV or less) or covered by default insurance. Furthermore, they operate from an extremely large capital base with the ability to spread their risk over a large number of mortgage loans and other investment vehicles.

Institutional subprime mortgage lenders also operate from a large capital base but without default insurance and the associated restrictions. Their qualification practices are more lenient, but they still have their limits.

Private lenders, on the other hand, are usually only concerned with the property and their equity position in it. They generally don't like going above 80% LTV. If they do, their rate and fees will be adjusted accordingly. These are typically wealthy individual investors, but by comparison, they are operating on a much smaller capital base. Their risk is spread over a small number of loans. The typical private lender likes to lend money out on small second mortgages between $20,000 and $50,000. For you, it's a good alternative for doing a refinance, raising some needed money without breaking your first mortgage.

I would like to point out that there are times when a private lender can be preferred (i.e., better terms) over an institutional subprime lender. In the aftermath of the 2008 credit crunch, the subprime market contracted and many subprime lenders disappeared. The few remaining subprime lenders have enjoyed their increased market share. It's simple supply and demand. With few subprime lenders to handle the demand, they are busy, which leads to higher rates and fees. You shouldn't overlook the alternative source of private funds. The good ones are happy to get the business and will price the loan fairly without gouging! A good full-service mortgage broker will have access to private money to check the fairness of any presented offers.

You may also be more interested in private money where the vendor in a purchase transaction is willing to take back a second mortgage. The vendor is usually more interested in completing the sale than getting a good interest rate and fee.

You will likely get better terms obtaining a mortgage through your family (love money) than a though subprime lender. Heck, you may even get better terms than a prime lender depending on how good a member of the family you have been.

If either you or the property doesn't conform to the conventional lending criteria at financial institutions (prime and subprime), you may require access to private funds. You are going to pay a higher rate of interest and additional fees. How much you pay will depend of the level of risk. Most borrowers today pay fees (mortgage broker fees and lender fees combined) between 2% and 4% of the mortgage amount. Private lenders generally don't pay the mortgage broker any commission like an institutional lender would for the business. Therefore, the mortgage broker must charge a fee for any services rendered. Interest rates could range between 8% and 15% depending on the loan's priority (i.e., first or second) and the overall risk with regard to borrower and property.

If you live in a small market, it's important to maintain good credit. I recently had a client with very good credit, but it became damaged quickly and her credit score dropped well below the prime lender's minimum score requirement. Without the benefit/protection of default insurance, subprime lenders must restrict their approved lending areas to bigger markets where properties can sell quicker if needed. Her only option was a private lender. Lucky for her, I knew an atypical private lender who lends outside his immediate area. Most private lenders like to be within driving distance of the property because they like to visit their collateral before making a decision and they are more familiar with local markets.

Bear in mind that private mortgage financing might only be for a short term. Perhaps the vendor wants to cash out in one year after taking back a mortgage so you could purchase the house, or maybe you need to re-establish credit this way. After one year of making payments on time, you will be in a better position to approach the mainstream lenders to refinance, assuming you have kept your record clean.

HIGH-YIELD INVESTMENT OPPORTUNITY

Private mortgages offer an alternative source of financing for borrowers and a high-yield investment opportunity for investors. Every consumer wants to invest their money wisely to maximize returns.

However, with increasing returns comes increasing risk. If you are going to invest in private mortgages, I strongly recommend you have a better than average understanding of the local real estate market you want to invest in, a very good understanding of your own tolerance to risk, and perhaps even the willingness to get involved with the administration end of your investment.

Poor underwriting procedures and inadequate security analysis have been the downfall of more than one private lender. A good mortgage broker has the expertise and resources to carry out these activities while keeping your long-term interests a priority. Given the higher level of risk, I approach each private mortgage application with the same or more rigour than a mortgage application destined for an institutional lender.

If you are less familiar with this kind of investment but want to get started, your mortgage broker can offer you some good advice to minimize your risk. For example, you should only lend against owner-occupied residential properties at a maximum 80% to 85% LTV, depending on the market. Owner-occupied properties are considered the least risky. In most cases, a borrower's principal residence is the last thing they will default on. No one wants to lose their home.

Also, you should hold the mortgage inside a self-directed RRSP so that you earn tax-free interest income. In addition, the plan and its trustee legally *must* receive its payments every month. If the borrower starts skipping payments, the matter is out of your hands. In plain English: the borrower is sued.

Finally, with comprehensive legislation in place for most provinces, such as the provisions of the *Mortgage Brokerages, Lenders and Administrators Act* in Ontario, you are certain to be provided all pertinent information regarding any mortgage investment. In Ontario, your mortgage broker is required to provide you with an investor/lender disclosure statement. Don't deal with any mortgage broker who doesn't provide this to you. It will put you at risk and the mortgage broker would be in breach of the act, which can (and should) lead to license revocation. This government form details all pertinent information about the transaction. Below are some of the included elements.

1. Conflict(s) of interest, including:
   - Does the mortgage broker expect to have a direct or indirect interest in the subject property?
   - Does a person related to the mortgage broker have a direct or indirect interest in the subject property?
   - Is the borrower related to the mortgage broker?
   - Is the individual or company that appraised the property related to the mortgage broker?

2. If the investment is to purchase an existing mortgage, is the mortgage now in default and has it been in default over the last twelve months?

3. What are the property's taxes and are the taxes in arrears?

4. Is the zoning on the property appropriate for the proposed use?

5. Has an appraisal been done? If so, what was the property's "as is" value?

The above is a small sample of the disclosure covered in the statement. In addition to providing the information in the aforementioned government form, effective January 1, 2009, Ontario mortgage brokerages are also required to provide a lender or investor with additional information in connection with this transaction. A brokerage must:

- advise you if the brokerage cannot verify the identity of another party to the transaction;

- disclose whether the brokerage is acting for the lender, the borrower, or both the borrower and lender;

- disclose to a lender the brokerage's relationship with each borrower, and disclose to an investor the brokerage's relationship with each party to the transaction;

- disclose whether the brokerage is receiving a fee or remuneration for referring you to a person or entity, and disclose the relationship with that person or entity;

- disclose material risks about the transaction that you should consider; and

- disclose actual or potential conflicts of interest that may arise from the transaction.

You must receive these disclosures in writing and acknowledge receipt of them at least two business days before you commit to lend/invest.

As with any good investment, you will make the best decision with full disclosure of all the facts. Without a doubt, the intention of the *Mortgage Brokerages, Lenders and Administrators Act* is to see that you are going into the investment with your eyes wide open and fully informed. The same goes for mortgage broker regulations in the other provinces. Just be sure your mortgage broker is licensed under the act and is in full compliance.

Conclusion

I wrote this book for two groups of people: the consumer and the mortgage broker apprentice. Both are looking to learn more about the business of getting a mortgage. I have worked in the mortgage industry for nineteen years and I am still learning the business. That's one of the things I like about it. I have tried to focus on the larger issues to help you get started. My hope is you will convert your new knowledge into savings and income respectively. The following is a summary of the key issues I want to underscore.

The banks have a number of distribution channels for originating new mortgage business. The mortgage broker channel is the banks' most cost-effective distribution system. For the aspiring or new mortgage broker, that represents great potential for an industry whose share of origination sits at around 30% to 40%. For the consumer, the upside is equally good: better mortgage terms and the independent representation needed to safely learn all the products and options available in the market. There is no reason not to think the mortgage broker market share can't keep growing until it gets to the U.S. level of 60% or 70% (pre-2008 credit crisis). Educating the public to better understand the business will be a key component to achieving that growth.

The Canadian mortgage industry is undergoing another paradigm shift. In the face of significant industry developments such as the 2008 credit crisis, industry consolidation, and price competition, many banks are starting to seriously evaluate the economics associated with the mortgage broker channel. As more lenders enter the business, the channel will remain a fixture in the Canadian mortgage distribution system, and Canadian mortgage holders will ultimately benefit from the increased product selection, value-added advice, and services that are more convenient.

However, mortgage brokers will also need to raise their game and meet the level of service sophistication that clients demand. Canadian homeowners now have increased access to mortgage rate information. No longer relevant are mortgage brokers who function as "rate shoppers." They are technologically savvy, hold the highest education and ethical standards in the industry, and are emerging as the predominant source of advice in the Canadian mortgage distribution system.

Continued investment in technologies will benefit consumers in terms of speed and convenience in obtaining a mortgage. The mortgage broker channel is a prime example of how to use technologies to interface with every party and every aspect associated with the process of arranging and registering a mortgage. Advances in digital technology have greatly improved the efficiency, consistency, accuracy, and reliability of the process. There are no longer any boundaries, such as geography or time of day, to restrict the interaction between client and mortgage broker.

I see consolidation in the mortgage broker channel continuing as a long-term trend. Increased competition, heightened compliance requirements, and rising technology costs have all pushed the smaller independent mortgage broker towards consolidation with superbrokerages. Today, 85% of Canadian mortgage brokers are employed by one of five superbrokerages. Nevertheless, there will always be a place for the smaller independents, just like there are always small efficient non-bank lenders. Mortgage brokers who can adapt to change, who have the innovation to exploit change, and who continue to stay focused on what really matters—putting client interests first—will survive.

Really get to know and understand your credit. Remember that many lenders now use auto-decision models built on minimum credit scores in their adjudication and rate setting process. It is therefore critical to understand your credit profile and take the necessary steps to optimize your credit rating before applying for a mortgage. I recommend checking your own credit report at least four months in advance of applying for a mortgage. If you need to work on improving your credit profile, talk to your mortgage broker in advance about the proactive steps you can take. You need at least two years of good credit history.

Purchasing a home is likely the most money you will ever spend at one time. The process involves working with a few trusted advisors, including a mortgage broker. Everyone in the industry has referrals at the ready. Getting a referral from someone you know and trust is a safe bet, but at some point, if not from the beginning, you may be working with people you've just met. Be sure to go in with your eyes open and ask many questions. Make sure the person you're dealing with is above board regarding the disclosure of compensation.

Finally, the time has come for me to stop complaining about the system for mortgage default insurance in this country and do something about it. I have started an online petition and I need your help if I am going to be successful in bringing about the necessary changes. A better system for mortgage default insurance, as I have described in this book, has been widely practiced in the U.S. for some time. It's time we stood up for ourselves and fought for a better deal. Please go to www.MortgageResource.ca/petition to sign the petition. I promise to do my part and deliver the message to the proper authorities.

ACKNOWLEDGEMENTS

Writing a book is not a solo project; there are many people I want to thank for making this project a success, starting with my absolutely indispensable office administrator, Cathy Cochrane. She runs the office and keeps me on top of everything. Thanks, Cathy.

Thanks to all the provincial regulators I contacted to get my facts straight on mortgage broker regulations across the country: Terri Robertson, Senior Registration Officer, Mortgage Broker Department, Financial Institutions Commission of British Columbia; Natalie Scollard, Communications Coordinator, Real Estate Council of Alberta; Mike Redler, Financial Institutions Officer, Saskatchewan Financial Services Commission; Bill Baluk, Registrar, The Manitoba Securities Commission; Claude Barsalou, Vice President, General Management, Organisme d'autoréglementation du courtage immobilier du Québec; Alaina Nicholson, Senior Enforcement Officer, Justice and Consumer Affairs, Government of New Brunswick; and John Corcoran, Department of Government Services, Financial Services Regulations Division, Government of Newfoundland and Labrador.

I also would like to thank the lawyers who provided clarity on specific charge terms associated with their province and their region: Pierre-Denis Leroux, Associé / Partner, McCarthy Tétrault

S.E.N.C.R.L., s.r.l., LLP, Montreal, Quebec, and Ian B. Bilek, Partner, Cox & Palmer, Halifax, Nova Scotia. Of course, special thanks to my trusted lawyer and friend, Peter Cass of Cass & Bishop, who has always been available to answer my legal questions when deals get complicated. Thank you, Peter, for reading my manuscript and for the complimentary foreword you provided.

Thank you to Canada Revenue Agency and Linda A. Neave, Business Development Officer, Canada Mortgage and Housing Corporation for clarifying the new HST rules regarding default insurance premiums.

Thank you to my publisher, Mike O'Connor at Insomniac Press, for giving me the opportunity to write my first book. I also want to thank my editor, Dan Varrette, for his sharp editorial skills, and all the other staff for their expert work.

Lastly, my deepest thanks to my wife, Michelle Schoots Anderson. You have supported my self-employed aspirations from day one in so many ways. And to our daughter, Sam, thanks for your support and encouragement. – Luvooga!

INDEX